BROKEN REVIVAL

AUTUMN WINCHESTER

Edited by
PINPOINT EDITING
Cover Designed by
JUST WRITE. CREATIONS

Copyright © 2017

by Autumn Winchester

All rights reserved. No part of this publication may be reproduced, distributed or transmitted in any form or by any means, including photocopying, recording, or other electronic or mechanical methods, without the prior written permission of the publisher, except in the case of brief quotations embodied in critical reviews and certain other noncommercial uses permitted by copyright law.

This is a work of fiction. Names, characters, places, and incidents are a product of the author's imagination.

AUTHOR'S NOTE

This novel has BDSM themes, mentions of abuse and rape, and contains slavery and crime.
This is not intended for anyone under the age of 18.

PROLOGUE

DAWN

Kneeling on the soft, red pillow, I awaited my Master to enter the playroom. My legs were shoulder width apart, my hands laced behind my back, my head down. I was naked, my waist length hair braided off to the side, no makeup to be seen. I took deep slow breaths, kneeling in the perfect pose—the pose he loved the most.

I had been to hell and back—more than once—but I was changed for the better.

I was beaten down to nothing and brought back, with no idea what had been done to me. Thanks to Master, I was made whole again. I was stronger in every way; no longer the timid girl he had saved from the darkness.

Although this was my first time in the playroom, I knew it like the back of my hand. I'd had to, so I could be ready for this moment.

This was new, exciting, and I was already wet with arousal, waiting for the fine combination of pleasure and pain I knew would be my undoing.

The floor squeak as he entered the room, igniting my nerves. I could feel his presence as he stepped over the threshold.

I held my breath as soft fingers ran over my hair in greeting.

He was hesitant, scared of causing me too much pain, but we both knew pain and pleasure went hand in hand when in the correct mind frame. I had picked out some toys that were familiar to me because we had used them in our bedroom. I had been preparing for this for weeks before we decided to come in here. I didn't think I would have any issues. I was certainly more excited than nervous.

I had chosen a blindfold, a bullet vibrator, and some silk rope. He called them beginner's objects numerous times.

"What is your safe word?" he asked softly, coming to a stop an inch in front of me. I could see his bare legs, knowing he wore only black silk boxers. I loved his nakedness, his tenderness, and everything else about him.

"Red," I said, just barely more than a whisper. "Green and yellow, also."

"Good girl," he said, petting my hair. It was hard, but I managed not to lean into him. He ran his hands up my legs, and I moaned as he began to massage my ass cheeks almost roughly.

"Are you wet for me?" he asked.

"Always for you, Sir," I moaned as he touched me, just between my legs, but not where I desperately wanted him.

"*Only* for me," he said, slipping the tip of his pinky into my wetness. I arched into him, wanting more.

"Please, Sir," I moaned, wanting more as he moved away.

"Soon," he said sweetly.

CHAPTER 1

DAWN

I should have been used to it by now, even with the numbness that had taken over, but the cold still lingered. Shadows danced behind my closed eyes. I was giving up. I knew my time was close to the end, and I was as ready as I could be to die. It wouldn't take much force to end my pathetic life. I'd lasted longer here than I thought I would.

My green eyes were sunken into my skull and my bones were barely covered by skin that was coated by grime. The nightgown I wore was nothing but rags. I could feel the fever from the virus forming within me. My roommate had fallen ill a few short days ago, and now it was only a matter of time before I lay among the dead—like her. I hoped it would be sooner rather than later.

Until last week, I had been completely by myself during my time here. I wasn't even sure where 'here' was. I just knew it was cold and dark—so freaking cold and dark—day and night.

I missed the sun upon my skin. I missed a loving touch. I missed *life*.

This hell was no place of happy memories, nor would it ever be.

"Let's go," barked an overweight guard as he noisily pulled opened the door to my jail cell. It made a grinding noise against the pebbled cement floor, making my ears ring.

I was in what is considered an isolation room in an underground jailhouse somewhere. There were no windows except for the little dirt covered one set in the door. A green, worn out cot sat against the far side of the room, next to a filthy metal toilet and sink. The sink had a small cup for drinking water, which was also dirty from my own hands. Who knew how long that cup had been around here? A flickering fluorescent light was fitted on the ceiling, but was hardly ever turned on.

My body was lying on its side and I could hardly move, even though I knew I had to. The air was thick. Mold and dirt clouded my senses and made breathing even more difficult. With blurry eyes, I watched the balding man stomp his way into the cell with a hard look on his face. I knew better than to disobey any command, but my body refused to work as the fever took hold. It made me weak; weaker than I had ever been during my time here.

Roughly, he grabbed my thin arm, right above my elbow on the rope burns from the day before and pulled me up. They were just another lasting scar upon my body. I scrunched my face in pain but didn't dare make a sound.

"You're lucky there's no time for a beating," he hissed as he dragged me out of the cell, as though I was nothing but a stuffed doll. I knew his Russian accent well. His breath smelled sour, and I tried to turn my face away as much as I could, so I didn't spill my guts on his shoes ... again.

The last time wasn't an incident I desired to remember.

I tried to keep up, but my legs could hardly hold the

weight of my ninety-pound body. The hall was just as damp and dirty as my cell. The air was slightly easier to breathe, but not much. Giving up the fight, I let my eyes close once again, not caring where I would end up. I prayed that wherever I did, it would end my wasted life.

"What's wrong with her?" spoke Master as we got to wherever we were going. His voice was raspy from his many years of smoking.

"I don't know," my handler grumbled as he let go of me. I fell awkwardly onto the filthy brown carpet. My face smashed into the floor as my arms refused to hold my weight. The rough fibers of the carpet poked against my cheek as I breathed in its puke-like smell.

Master Galvin, a deadly man, walked into my personal space, demanding my attention. My unfocused eyes stared at shiny black shoes. I knew his black hair would be greasy and hanging down to the top of his eyebrows. He was just below six feet tall, and never had a wrinkle out of place in his clothes. It didn't matter if he wore a perfect expensive suit or his workout clothes—he always carried himself as though everyone was supposed to bow down to him, and him alone.

He was verbally kinder than the men he bossed around, and never lifted a hand to me, but that didn't mean he was nice. Not by a long shot. He may have never physically harmed me, but that never stopped him from causing me harm. Master was always able to get his men to do it instead.

"Poor child," Master mumbled as he felt my forehead with the back of his chilled hand. "Morgan, go get some OxyContin so she can at least be auctioned. Tess didn't make it, and I'm sure she has the same virus as the others. Let's try to keep her alive long enough to make some money from her."

"Yes Sir," said Morgan with a slight nod of his head, before he walked heavily out of the room.

I knew exactly where every piece of furniture was in this

office—I had been here countless times. A beat-up oak desk sat in the middle of the room with two white foldable chairs facing it. A small kitchen area was to the left, while the right side of the room held boxes of files. The walls were covered in wood paneling and the lighting was bright, the lamps in the two corners filling the room with glare.

"You have given me great service, but I'm afraid I no longer have a need for you. Your age is causing issues amongst my men. I'm sure someone will want you; I know my son does, but I can't let him have a gift as sweet as you until he learns his place. Selling you tonight is my only option. That is, of course, if you survive this illness," Master spoke quietly from above me as he brushed the sweaty hair off my face in a fatherly manner.

Had he purposely caused me to get this sick? I certainly wouldn't put it past him. I wasn't worth much to this man— never was. I was just a means to an end like the rest of girls.

"It saddens me greatly to have to make this choice. It was a pleasure to train you, but your mother will now have her debts forgiven."

"Here you are, Sir," Morgan spoke loudly as he walked back into the room.

My head was pounding with each heartbeat. I could feel each breath I took, pounding through my skull like a drum.

"Perfect!" Master Galvin slapped his thigh before holding his hand out for the syringe. "This will make the pain go away long enough for you to be bought by the highest bidder. It will make you sleep for a few hours. So, unfortunately, I won't be getting as much as I would like," he continued as he pushed the needle into my thigh, administering the drug into my system. The small prick was nothing compared to the torture I'd already suffered. "It is a shame. So many men like having a trained slave."

I could feel the drug's effect all too soon. Some of the soreness began to creep away as Morgan once again pulled me to my feet. I was at least able to hold myself erect somewhat now, even if my eyes didn't want to stay open any longer. He none-to-gently pulled me behind him as we left the office and entered back into the stained hallway.

We passed through a few different rooms and went down hallways I had never seen. Most of the rooms were either totally empty or filled with boxes stacked haphazardly.

We finally came to a stop in a room where other girls were either standing in the waiting position, or being held by a rope around their necks as they kneeled beside their own handlers. The room was the size of Master's office, but not any cleaner. The paint was peeling off the walls, and the floor had stains from previous occupants. I had never been to this part of the building before today.

Another man, one I couldn't recall seeing before now, slapped a piece of paper with large black numbers onto my ugly gown. I would have fallen if Morgan hadn't kept me from doing so—although he did laugh.

Why was he so amused by my reactions? I couldn't help being weak. Maybe if they'd given me more food to survive in this hell, I'd be a bit stronger.

I vaguely watched through blurry eyes with my head down as the slaves were moved from the room in groups through another door. Most of the girls struggled as they were dragged out, some crying and fighting against their restraints.

I had once been like them. I once thought that struggling and fighting would be the key to getting out of this place, but all it did was cause more pain. All it did was cause more lasting bruises from the inside out.

I didn't think I'd ever heal from such abuse. I'd likely die in pain.

"I was trying to talk Galvin into letting me have you, or even taking you until you got over your illness, but he wouldn't allow me," Morgan whispered in my ear, kneeling at my level so no one would be able to hear him. His breath was too warm against my heated skin. "You are wonderful in every way, my Pet. I will find you and bring you home when the time comes. I promise I will be the best Daddy to you." He roughly kissed my cheek and grabbed my breast before he backed away. I took a deep breath, trying not to let his touch get to me. I was unable to hold in the shiver that wracked my body, unsure if it was from the spoken words or from his touch—most likely from both.

Morgan dragged me through the door when my number was called, along with several others. I stumbled up the few steps that led to a wooden stage. I couldn't see much through the smoke and bright lights that were pointed towards the platform. Some of the girls were crying, while one or two had gags in their mouths.

Once on the stage, I was forced to stay still after Morgan tapped against the back of my knees with his foot. I didn't pay attention to what was said as each girl was auctioned. I kept my position, kneeling on the floor, hands behind my back and chest jutting out. I knew most of the girls were either tied with their hands behind them so they had less of a chance of trying to run. Most of these girls had not been held captive for as long as I had. They had no idea how deadly these men were. I still didn't know everything they were capable of doing.

When my turn came, I was forced forward to a podium where a man stood wearing a black suit. I kept my head down, arms behind my back, knowing I would easily be punished if I was out of line in any way. I was sure my body wouldn't be able to take any more pain—not right now.

Although, on second thought, maybe that would finally end my pathetic life.

"Number 73. Age nineteen. About five foot two. She's ill, so she is unable to perform any service tonight after purchase. She is fully trained, and can do every command you wish her to do. Let's start the bidding at ten grand," spoke the man with a foreign accent.

I was unable to follow the fast pace the bidding took. The man spoke too fast and I kept swaying, trying not to allow the dizziness at the edge of my vision to take over.

"Sold to paddle number 109," the man said, as I was shoved sideways towards the other end of the stage, where I practically fell down the steps. Once down, I was guided towards a wall as my eyes began to stay closed on their own accord.

"Remember, she's drugged just a tad and already falling asleep. She won't be of any service until the drugs are out of her system," my handler spoke. "She is completely trained and ready to be at your service within twelve hours."

A different hand that I didn't recognize, much gentler than the hands to which I had grown accustomed, touched my upper arm as I nearly fell, almost falling into the man that now owned me. Morgan once again laughed as the new man gently, but sternly, led me out of the building after making sure I was stable enough to walk on my own.

It was dark outside, and I gave up the fight as the drugs took over my body. Letting my legs carry me wherever I was led, I hardly felt the rough ground against my bare feet as we made our way outside into the night. I could have been walking over hot, sharp glass for all I knew. I didn't really care.

CHAPTER 2

ELIJAH

Sometimes, I hated my job. I loved the money, don't get me wrong, but I hated the things I had to do—who I had to pretend to be. After faking my identity so many times, sometimes I couldn't remember who the real me *was*.

Some mornings, I'd ask myself *"Who am I today?"*, just to make sure I remembered who I needed to pretend to be. Thankfully, I was able to see my family, claiming them as my employees when required.

My current identity was one I had been working under for well over a year. I had yet to find the evidence I needed. I wasn't sure I ever would. It was nearly impossible when I didn't even really know what was needed. I knew the goal was to bring down one of the most popular group of men that supported sex trafficking, but it was a lot easier said than done.

Once this job was finished, I would be taking one heck of a break.

I wanted to be anywhere else, but I didn't have a choice.

When I got that phone call this morning, inviting me to the auction, I had to accept. It could lead me to some much needed information, I had been waiting a very long time to get. I needed more proof and more information to bring down this organization. This could very well be my chance—my chance to finally bring this case to a close.

I had to do this one step at a time, no matter how long it.

I *would* bring down this sex slave ring, and save as many innocent people as I could in the process. I just hoped that I could get it done sooner rather than later.

I didn't know what to expect as I got out of my car, fifteen minutes before the auction would take place. I wasn't too gentle with shutting the car door, either. Most of the cars in the parking lot were rentals, with a few pricey cars in the mix. I knew most of these people who would be here tonight, and they had a huge amount of money to waste. They wanted no lasting ties when they left—and there wouldn't be.

Each man here knew the risks and took such measures to keep those low, so any law enforcement agent could not trace anything to them personally. Even the CIA had been kept away. Of course, I wouldn't put it past some of the agents to be working undercover, just like me. Some were likely to be being paid to turn a blind eye.

I nodded and made small talk to a few men as I walked towards the opened door of the nondescript building downtown. I would guess many of these men did odds and ends like myself to prove their trustworthiness. I started out with selling drugs, hiding inventory, and a few other petty things. I proved myself by letting Galvin think I was able to get information to him from my workplace to keep his affairs safe. I did everything a newbie wannabe would do—all but the killing part. That went against not only my code of conduct, but also my beliefs.

Little did he know that I would be the one and only

person to bring all his hard work crashing down in ashes soon enough.

"Welcome, Mr. Hunter," greeted the bouncer, who was dressed in all black. I was surprised he remembered my name, as we'd only met once, months ago. The man was all muscle, with scars lining his body.

"Wilson," I nodded at him. He still had the shaved head and goatee, a huge contrast to his pale white skin. He was a guard for a purpose, and one I didn't feel like fighting if I didn't have to. I was big but he was twice my size, and I was big.

I entered the building, where many of the men were smoking like chimneys. I tried to suppress my cough as I looked around the room. A stage was towards the back of the room with lights shining brightly towards it. A podium stood on one end.

I made small talk with a few men while I grabbed a numbered paddle and found a spot so I would be able to see the stage. I nodded to my partner, who was a few paces away. He had a beanie over his hair, but he wore his workout clothes, not caring what others thought of him.

I didn't plan to purchase anything, as I didn't want the hassle of having to deal with issues that would come with buying – and I used that term loosely — one of these so-called slaves. I would bid to make it look like I was interested, but nothing more.

A high-pitched whistle sounded through the room, and the men grew quiet with anticipation as a line of girls was dragged onto the stage at the same time a man took a stance behind the podium.

"Welcome, gents!" greeted the man. He wore all black, just like the bouncer and the handlers of these girls. He was slightly skinnier than Wilson, who stood at the front door, but had a full head of hair. I gathered they were at least related somehow. "We have one hundred and thirty-two servants to

BROKEN REVIVAL

auction tonight. There is no system to how they are to be sold. Like usual, I will tell you the height, age, and a little about their personalities and training status. Now, let's begin!" He was too happy, doing what was expected of him.

The line of girls was roughly handled as they were each auctioned one at a time. The sold girl was then led off the stage and towards a small table where another man sat, watching with a gleeful look. Each girl was forced to her knees while they waited their turn to be claimed by their new owner. The new owner who paid cash before taking ownership.

Line after line was brought out to the stage. Most were filthy from head to toe with bruises on their bodies. Most of these girls were runaways, and no one would ever be looking for them, since they had aged out of the system. The girl my brother had rescued was a runaway from an abusive boyfriend, and had been in even worse shape than most of these girls.

It wasn't until group seven that one girl in particular caught my attention. She was just like the rest: dirty from head to toe, tangled black hair, and so boney her skin barely concealed her pain. She kept swaying back and forth, and could hardly keep herself upright. I couldn't get a good look at her face as she took her spot on the stage.

Her handler kicked the back of her knees, making her fall. I expected a cry of shock to come from her, but she remained quiet and distant to the whole affair. To me, that was not normal. Just comparing her to the other girls that had been on that stage so far, she was different—and not in a good way.

I kept my eyes on her, and when it was her turn to be auctioned, I knew what I had to do. The gut feeling demanded my attention. I knew that if I didn't follow it, I'd be beating myself up for who knew how long.

"Number 73. Age nineteen. About five foot two. She's ill, so she is unable to perform any service tonight after purchase.

She is fully trained. Let's start the bidding at ten grand," said the auctioneer.

I slowly raised my paddle. A few people around me also rose their paddles. The bidding wore didn't last long, as most of these men didn't want to deal with a sick purchase. So, after a few short minutes, I won, paying the total of twenty thousand dollars. I could easily pay that for the girl who looked like she was giving up on life.

I could feel Erick, Galvin's son, glaring daggers at me, but ignored him. Erick was always all talk and no bite—just another druggy who wanted his fix in any form he could get it.

I filled out the form, confirming I had read the rules and knew I would not be able to return the girl—not that I would dream of doing so. I handed over the cash to the man, hardly taking notice of him in my anxiety to see the girl's face.

"Remember, she won't be of any service until the drugs are out of her system," the handler stated. "She is completely trained, and ready to be at your service tomorrow."

The girl fell into me, face first, as she took the last step down from the stage. As she continued to sway, I gently laid a hand on her upper arm. Ignoring the men that were watching, I began to lead the girl out of the building. Once outside, I scooped her up into my arms before making my way to the car. There was no way I was going to make her walk barefoot over the gravel and broken glass in the parking lot. She hardly weighed anything and as her head flopped onto my shoulder, it almost felt like it fit there.

Like she fit into my life.

Her skin was hot, a slight sheen of sweat covering her skin from head to toe.

I juggled her in my arms so I could dig my keys out of my pocket once I got to the car. I gently sat the sleeping girl in the passenger seat and covered her with my jacket. I buckled her seatbelt over it so it wouldn't slip off her—with it being late October, the night air was cooling quickly.

It was a long two-hour drive back home and she slept soundlessly, except for the occasional wheeze or cough. I couldn't help but keep glancing over at her.

Could it be her? After five years, it didn't seem likely.

When we arrived at my house, I carried her to the room she would be able to call her own. I wasn't sure what I was doing, or what I would need to do, but I knew just the person to ask.

CHAPTER 3

DAWN

We are born into this world as equals. Once we take our first breath, we depend on our parents to take care of us, to keep us alive by giving us the food and shelter we need. There are so many people who want children but are unable to carry any, while so many people are gifted a child and want nothing to do with it. Then, there are the people who would give their children the clothes off their own backs if needed.

When I was young, my parents worked hard to make sure I had everything I needed. Dad worked at a supermarket at night, while Mom worked for a cleaning company during the day. Growing up, I didn't know how poor we really were. Neither did I know who my parents truly were as people. I was a small child, and they were loving parents, no matter what they chose to do.

I didn't have the same things that other kids my age, and I never asked why. I just thought that was how it was.

When my dad was murdered at his job one fateful night,

my life changed forever. I was eleven when my mom began to work more shifts at the cleaning service—or so she said. Little did I know at the time that she was getting into something she would never be able to stop. She became distant, and I began to take care of myself.

The night I turned fourteen, I was taken out of my home by a man I thought I could trust. A man I thought was halfway decent compared to many of the other men who hung around my mom. Mom was at work that night, so I allowed him into the apartment, since he had popped up a few times a week for a while. Besides, he brought food, and I was starving. I never thought he'd be one of those men who turned out to be my worst nightmare. It was my birthday, after all. I hadn't thought anything was awry until it was too late.

Looking back, I wish I knew how much of a monster he was. I wish I could turn back time and then maybe things would have ended much differently. All this was because one stupid man thought he deserved to dabble with my life.

I was at the sink before we were going to eat, filling up the green plastic cups with water, when he came up behind me. He grabbed me around my neck, nearly choking me in the process. The cup bounced along the floor as it fell from my grip, water splashing my feet. I didn't realize this man could be so cruel. I knew he had some dirty thoughts, just by the way he would look at my mom, and how he said things with a glint in his eye. However, I was only fourteen and a virgin; I didn't realize then how evil men could be.

I struggled against him, kicking and screaming. I did everything I'd been taught to do. I bit the hand he placed over my mouth in an attempt to silence my screams. My heart beat fast and hard in my chest as fear consumed me. I hastily used a chair to block his path when I got away from him, and then I ran, my feet taking me away from him on their own accord.

It didn't deter him long, as he caught me when I reached

the door, grabbing me around my midsection. He then poked a needle into my neck.

When I awoke some time later, I was in a dark, damp cell. The walls were filthy from who knew what. Surprisingly, I didn't cry or yell. I just sat there quietly, lost in my own mind. Looking back, I was probably in shock. I waited for someone to come kill me. That would have saved me a lot of pain. I often wished for death to take me during the years I was there. I still wish it today.

For over five years I was held underground. I was forced into submission, molded into someone I didn't want to be. It became harder and harder as the days passed to remember who I really was. I lost my mind, my dignity, and my body.

The clothes I wore were no longer mine. I slept on a cot until it broke, and then I slept on the cold cement floor with nothing to fend off the cold that permeated the air. After so long, my body became numb to the horrors and abuse. I gave up hoping I'd ever get out of that place. I no longer had any fight left in me. There was no point.

Waking up warm and lying on what felt like a cloud frightened me as much as waking to complete darkness. My body was sore; my throat on fire, as though I had swallowed sandpaper. My head thumped with each beat of my heart. I felt the warmth of the sunlight shine upon my face through the crack in the curtain. I wanted to open my eyes, to see the sun, but I was too afraid.

Everything hurt—even the blood pulsing through my veins.

Please, death. Take me!

The floor creaked as someone entered the room. I tried to keep my breathing even as footsteps came closer. Of course, when a warm hand touched my forehead, I jumped a mile, instantly sitting up and trying to move as far as I could from the person, almost flinging my body away from the touch. No one had touched me so gently in years.

Not realizing how small a bed I was on, I ended up falling off, hard onto the floor. I threw my hands behind me, but my wrists hurt and I groaned out in discomfort.

"Well, good morning," said a man as he walked around the bed. His voice was filled with concerned humor. He had short, dark brown hair that had a natural curl to it. His heart-shaped face had some stubble growing. My eyes refused to move from his as his dark eyes, so much so, that I couldn't look away.

What was he going to do? Who was he?

"You still have a fever, girl," he said kindly as he kneeled next to me, ignoring the way my body flinched. My eyes were wide as I stared at him. He slowly moved his hand to my upper arm and I jerked away from his touch once more. I couldn't help the response my body made because of the years of abuse. "You need rest," he said.

Although I was frightened, his voice was calm—nearly the type of calm that might easily put me to sleep, though

Too tired and confused, I didn't fight as the man gently lifted me and laid me back on the bed. He handed me a bottle of water, which I gladly gulped half of right away, not caring that some spilled down my chin.

"For now, you are to rest. I want you to sleep as much as you can. The bathroom is the open door across the room." He pointed to the direction of the bathroom and I followed the line of sight. "You're welcome to use the shower to get clean. I'll bring some food soon, as well. Once you're feeling better, I'll go over the rules of this house and what I expect from you," he said quietly but firmly, in a way I knew to obey. He handed me one red pill, Advil, and I swallowed it without question.

"I put some clothes on the counter. I'll be back in a little bit to check on you and change your sheets," he said.

After he left, I looked around the room. I sat on the bed. On either side of the bed stood nightstands. A door across the room most likely led to the hallways, which was next to one of the bookshelves.

Slowly, I got up off the bed and made my way towards the bathroom, craving a warm shower. I was only allowed to bathe once a month at the place I was kept, if I was lucky, and in cold water. Not the best of options, but at least I did get a chance to be clean somewhat.

This bathroom was huge with a heated floor.

I wondered if I had died, because there was no possible way I'd ever see something this grand anywhere.

I stripped my dirty gown from my body before turning on the water. Once the water was warm—almost too warm—I stepped in and closed the glass door. The water poured over me, washing the filth away.

It *felt* like heaven. I could die here and never complain.

Spotting the shampoo, I began to wash my hair. I washed my entire body and hair over and over until the water ran clean. I also put a bunch of conditioner in my hair, hoping to lessen the tangles. I hadn't had a brush or comb in years.

When the water grew cold, I sadly shut it off and wrapped a fluffy white towel around me. I put on the pair of gray yoga pants and black shirt that were lying on the counter. They were big, but clean and warm; a lot better than that filthy gown I was forced to wear over the last three years.

"I'll brush your hair while we talk a little," a voice said as I was putting the towel back on the hook by the shower.

I jumped at his voice, my heart doubling in speed. How long had he been there? Had he watched me take a shower? What would he want from me?

"I just got here," he said quickly when he saw my frightened eyes. "Now, come take a seat, please." He went and sat on the bed, which now had clean sheets and a green checkered comforter folded back.

Schooling my face, I ignored the mirror as I walked back into the room, keeping my head down. My wet hair dripped down my back. The man sat on the bed, towards the middle, so I had more than enough room to sit in front of him on the floor. He had a brush in his hand that he was playing with as he watched me.

"Come sit," he demanded gently as he tapped the spot in front of him.

I obeyed, stiff and unsure. I was used to knowing what to expect in my predictable ugly life. I had known I would be abused, yelled at, and forced to do things I never thought I would ever have to do.

"I won't hurt you," he said as I sat in front of him. He put a soft warm towel around my shoulders and slowly began to brush my black hair, being extremely gentle with the tangled mess. "I used to brush my sister's hair quite often.

"What's your name?" he asked, almost too quiet for me to hear.

"Dawn, Sir," I answered in a hoarse voice as I stared blankly at the wall across the room.

"Dawn what?" he prompted.

"Dawn Ellis, Sir," I half whispered, half cried, expecting the punishment I would have endured from Master Galvin.

"No need to cry, sweet girl," he whispered as he leaned in towards my hair. "I wasn't clear about what I wanted. You won't be punished for my mistake. You won't ever be punished cruelly in my house." Moving back, he continued the work on my hair. "I am Elijah Brown, but if anyone asks, it's Elijah Hunter. You are to address me as Sir, or Elijah, or even Mr. Hunter, unless otherwise told.

"You are welcome to take a shower every day if you'd like," he finished, beginning to braid my hair. His voice was quiet and calm.

Being in the company of a man for so long usually meant he would demand my services in some sort of fashion. I wasn't the best at some of the things the men wanted from me, but I everything in my power to keep them happy, no matter what. That way, I had less punishment on most days. This man—Elijah—didn't seem to want anything from me.

"All done," Elijah said with a smile in his voice. He slowly got up off the bed and I automatically ducked my head down. I wasn't allowed to make eye contact without permission. I heard him sigh as though he were disappointed about something.

"You still have a fever, Dawn," he said as he felt my forehead with the back of his hand. "Get in bed. Rest. Try to sleep some more. I will bring some soup up in a bit."

I nodded as I hastily moved to the bed and laid my head down on the pillow. He smiled sadly at me. "You obey very well. Now rest." He made sure I was tucked in before dimming the lights and leaving the room, keeping the door cracked open an inch. Tears suddenly filled my eyes because of the care he had shown me.

I can't trust him. I can't trust any man.

My eyes closed on their own, much easier than I'd thought they would. I'd never been allowed to sleep so much, no matter how sick I was. I'd only really been sick a few times while I'd been held in the cell, and never this bad. My entire body hurt. I could feel my body wanting to cough, but I did my best to not allow it, so I wouldn't draw attention to myself.

Attention was never a good thing in my life.

CHAPTER 4

ELIJAH

*P*lopping down in my black leather chair, I held my head in my hands. The girl, Dawn, was so lost to the pain and abuse she'd suffered. I could tell she had no idea how much pain she held inside of herself. I wasn't sure how long she'd been in that awful place, but I knew it was longer than any of the other girls. From her submissive personality and reactions, it would be a hard road to get her to not be so withdrawn. I would do everything in my power to help her find out who she could become.

She still had a fever, and I'd given her Motrin. If her temperature wasn't down by the end of the day, I'd be calling my father to come check on her. I'd have to call him soon anyway, so I could get a checkup done and her injuries documented. He was the only man I could trust to give Dawn the health care she needed to survive.

Taking her to a hospital was out of the question. With her most likely tagged as a runaway like many of the other slaves, it would bring up flags when her name was entered into their database. I didn't want her taken away—she would be safer with me.

However, her health had to be documented down to a T. It had to be to bring her abusers into custody with charges. Any little thing would add to their sentence, and this case could come to a close.

While Dawn took a shower, I changed the sheets on her bed and called my mother. I didn't have a whole lot of food she'd be able to eat. I was hardly ever at home lately, with my demanding job.

Groaning, I opened the FBI database on my Mac and entered her name into the search engine. I hoped beyond hope that she wasn't who I was thought she was, and I hoped beyond hope that she was, and I had found her. If she was my Dawn, I had no idea what I would do.

～

DAWN

A few hours later, I was awoken by someone sitting beside me on the bed, smoothing my hair back from my forehead. Groggily, I opened my eyes and saw a blurry Elijah. I blinked again, not understanding why he'd woken me up. Did he want me to service him? If so, why couldn't he just stick his dick wherever he wanted it?

"Time to rise and shine," he smiled. "My mother is getting a bowl of soup ready for you."

Huh?

I pushed myself into a sitting position, wrapping my arms around my knees. The lamp closest to me was on, making a soft glow around the room. It was dark outside as I looked through the slight opening of the curtain-covered window.

"I would have woken you up sooner, but you looked so peaceful."

I remained silent, looking at the place my toes were under the covers as I tried to keep my tears at bay. My throat felt like it was on fire, and my body like I had been run over by a truck . . . three times or more. I was afraid of what was going to happen to me. When would he quit being kind?

"Are you feeling any better?" Elijah asked, ducking his head down to try and meet my eyes.

I closed them and shook my head. I felt worse, like death was knocking on the door, but at least my head wasn't pounding right now. My throat was still sore and my chest felt like an elephant was sitting on it.

"As of right now, I recommend lots of rest until you're better. Your fever isn't as high, but you kept coughing while you slept. After you eat, I have some medication you can take. It'll hopefully kick this bug out of your system." He laid a hand softly over my own.

This time, my body didn't jerk at his touch.

"Hello, dear," greeted a woman as she came strolling into the room. I kept my position, but saw her frown from the edge of my vision. Her clothes were simple for this late hour. "I wasn't sure what you liked, so I made one of Elijah's favorite soups. I didn't bring much up, just to be sure you liked it." She handed me the steaming bowl.

Slowly, I moved my arms from around my knees. I grabbed the blue plastic bowl tighter than needed, afraid it would be taken away from me. Morgan would do that constantly, and I learned to just wait it out most of the time.

"Thank you, ma'am," I whispered, looking up at her through my eyelashes. She had shoulder length light brown hair, and warm green eyes. Her face was familiar, but I couldn't place where I may have seen her before. With my cloudy thinking, I probably wouldn't be able to anytime soon.

"Oh, none of that nonsense. Call me Joslyn," the woman smiled warmly.

I nodded before I began to eat the food, trying not to gulp

it down. The soup was warm and soothing along my dry, scratchy throat, and the bowl heated up my chilled hands as I ate.

"Joslyn is my adoptive mother," Elijah explained. "She will be staying here with you tomorrow while I have a few meetings I have to attend. I expect you to rest."

"Yes, Sir," I answered as I finished off the bowl of soup.

"Here is another Motrin and some Nyquil, which will hopefully let you sleep better. We don't want to give you an antibiotic until the doctor checks you out. Joslyn will be here when you wake up, and I will check on you a few more times," Elijah said, taking the empty bowl from my hands with ease. He took enough care to not touch me more than he needed.

"Okay," I said through a yawn once I'd swallowed the medicine. Joslyn then helped me to lie down and tucked me back into the bed. It didn't take long for my body to sink into the mattress in oblivion.

ELIJAH

I had explained to my mother as much as I could about the girl who would be staying in my home. I'm sure she didn't entirely believe me, but didn't push. Of course, I had to make her promise to not let slip in any way that I was working undercover. I knew my parents would be safe, since Galvin wouldn't be able to tie anyone to me from the documents I'd forged. Having friends in low places was always a bonus—even if it was against FBI protocol.

I had to do what had to be done if my boss wanted this ring of felons to be brought down.

Dawn Ellis' father had been good friends with my parents until his death seven years ago. Dawn and her parents had been to my parents' home many times before they'd moved, shortly before the death of Quentin, her father.

Dawn used to look up to me. Now, she had no one to look to for help except me.

I hated the idea of leaving her alone, so I gladly let my mom keep an eye on her for a few hours after she insisted on helping. I knew the poor girl was confused, and being so sick on top of it didn't help matters.

Once at the office, I briefly explained to Zack and Kaleb, my bosses, about my findings, along with giving them the papers I'd had my father put together as her tending physician. The fewer people who knew about what was going down, the better. I knew there was at least one leak in this office, and I didn't want word to get out more than necessary.

We sat in one of the smaller conference rooms. The three of us sat around the table as I told the full story of how I'd come across Dawn. It was difficult to keep my tone even as I described what I'd found so far.

I was surprised by what I'd found when I'd searched for her in the database. The girl had been kidnapped from her home while her mother worked the night shift. It was Dawn's fourteenth birthday—one that would never be forgotten. The house was a disaster, showing signs of a struggle.

There were no leads to who had taken her, or where she could possibly be. Knowing where I found her, I could only imagine what kind of abuse she'd suffered through. She'd been missing without a trace for over five years.

I read through the interviews of her mother, mother's boyfriend, and the neighbors, but no one knew anything about what had happened. They each had clear alibis, and no one was considered a suspect.

She was the main reason I'd trained to be an FBI agent. Since I'd graduated high school a year early and then college in three years, I was one of the youngest ever to enter Quantico. I wanted to make a difference to the young children and women who went missing every day with no leads, no suspects.

I was good at what I did, and everyone around me knew it, too.

"I think you should be taken off this case," Kaleb said, looking at me with his gray eyes. His look sometimes unnerved even me. It wasn't like he could read my thoughts, but it sure felt like it more than once. "I'll move you to a safe house and take Dawn into another one across the country."

"Absolutely not," I stated, anger boiling at just the thought. "I can't just leave, or they'll know something's up. You know that as well as anyone else. Plus, she's too sick to go anywhere."

"But you know her," Kaleb glared at me. I wasn't going to back down. I had to stay. It didn't matter that I knew her, or that she was not the same girl I had once known. She was still a part of me—part of this case.

"I'll be fine. I'm not backing down on this case. I've worked way too much on it for you to just drop me off like trash," I seethed. "I've spent the last year gaining my spot inside this ring, Kaleb! I can't just let it pass on by without me, now that I'm in this deep."

"Fine. But if your emotions get involved, you will be shipped out, got it?" Kaleb didn't remove his eyes from mine.

"Yes, Sir," I said. I hated how he could bring me, a Dom, down into a submissive place.

CHAPTER 5

DAWN

A week passed where I was in and out of sleep. Every time I woke—mostly in a coughing fit—either Elijah or Joslyn were there, comforting me. I was so used to taking care of myself that I always expected to wake back up in the cell.

I kept having dreams of what I'd been forced to live through over and over. The times I woke up coughing, the two made sure I could catch my breath before having me drink warm tea and honey.

By the fifth day, my fever and sore throat were getting worse. The coughing also seemed to grow worse by the hour, and so did my nightmares. Everything began to blur together. I could no longer tell the difference between my dreams and reality.

On day eight, I woke up by myself, finally being able to breathe without hacking up a lung. The dull sunlight lit the room and the window was open, letting in fresh air. I could faintly hear voices out in the hall.

I stretched my stiff body out, happy I was no longer achy. I was tired but felt more rested—more human. It had been years since I'd actually *felt* human. I wasn't sure how to take it.

I could feel my hair sticking to my face and neck. I was too scared to get up or move too much, as I wasn't sure what was expected of me, even though the idea of a shower was at the front of my mind.

As I brought my hand up to my face to rub my crusted eyes, I noticed I had a needle taped into my vein on the back of my hand. The movement caused it to pull slightly. *When did that happen?*

"Sorry about the IV," Elijah said as he entered the room, wearing a pair of gray sweatpants and a dark blue shirt. He looked tired but seemed to be happy I was awake. "I had my father look you over a couple days ago, since you weren't getting better. He started an IV full of fluids and antibiotics for pneumonia and strep throat. With how you lived for so long, he was surprised you weren't worse, but was also afraid of how fast you could go downhill without the proper treatment.

"Since you're on the mend, my father can remove the IV, but you'll still have to take meds until the infection is gone. You can take a shower and get some food afterward."

"Okay, Sir," I said, my voice scratchy from lack of use.

"Good to see you awake, child," greeted a man with black hair. His face was open and warm as he looked me over. His light blue eyes shone with trust and compassion. I felt like I'd met this man before.

"How are you feeling?" he asked as he took hold of my wrist, checking my heart rate before proceeding to remove the IV. He was gentle as he removed it and put a Band-Aid on the spot. He didn't touch me more than necessary, for which I was thankful.

"Better, Sir," I said, trying to keep my eyes down from his.

"Good to hear," the man smiled. He retreated a few steps, giving me more than enough room to be able to get up. I could feel him staring at me. I had to wonder why—why did he feel obligated to even treat me?

"Go take a shower. I'll get some clothes for you while you're in there and set them on the counter. When you're done, I will do your hair, and then you will eat some food," Elijah said gently, before he stood and let me get up. His voice wasn't demanding or stern, but calm and open. I was used to how roughly men usually spoke to me, and it was a nice change—as long it was kept that way, which I doubted.

I slowly made my way off the bed, trying my best to ignore the worried eyes watching me. I noticed my clothes were different than the ones I had last had on. The shorts were a little too big, but they were cute with white and pink hearts. The tank top fit me perfectly. I had to wonder who'd changed me. I knew my body was covered in scars. Did that mean whoever changed my clothes saw them?

My bare feet touched the soft cream carpet, as I worked to keep myself upright. It wasn't anything I couldn't handle; I had suffered pain on a daily basis. It took me a little longer to get moving, but at least I could do so without help for the most part. Elijah did follow, silently, obviously to make sure I didn't fall.

Once I reached the bathroom, I relieved myself, as my bladder had made itself painfully known. After the water had warmed up, I stepped in the shower and cleaned my body from head to toe. It felt just as great as the last time.

This was one thing I could certainly get used to.

Once I finished and felt much more like my old self, I found the clothes Elijah had put on the counter: a simple matching bra and underwear set, along with dark pink yoga pants that had a flower design along the side. There was also a light pink tank top and a long-sleeved shirt to put over it.

Elijah, once again, sat on the bed like last time. He smiled gently, almost sadly in a way, as I reached the bed. I sat on the edge as well, too worn out to keep my body on alert, letting my shoulders sag.

He began to brush out my wet hair. It wasn't as tangled, as it had still been in a braid from before. I found it soothing once again, and would have purred if I had the ability.

Why was he so nice?

"All done," he stated after he had once again braided my hair in a French twist.

"Thank you, Sir," I replied.

"Not a problem," he muttered. "Now, how 'bout we go downstairs and eat some food." He made his way off the bed, and I followed, knowing the statement was more a command than anything else. He entwined his hand gently with mine and led me downstairs.

The hallway was lined with beautiful pictures of nature. I didn't stop to look too closely, but would love to if I got the chance. I had no idea what this man had planned for me. He could very well turn around and sell me again, since I was now healthy. Well, healthier than I was when he bought me.

The carpet, the same cream color as the bedroom, was soft and clean against my feet. In the house I grew up in, the carpet was dirty, no matter how hard my mother tried to clean it. Some of the threads would poke the bottoms of my feet if I l stepped just right. Not to mention, the bare spots would easily cut my soles.

I followed the man down the wide stairs that led to an open entryway with more pictures, and a sort of western style table near the main doors. A few of the pictures were of nature: a tree in a dry field, mountains, and a sunset. I had never seen such art before.

"This way," he stated, rounding the corner towards the right.

I came into what was a massive kitchen. It looked like it came right out of a show home.

"Go sit," he said, as he nodded towards the round oak table that seated four, and let go of my hand at the same time. The chairs were high backed and fitted with dark red cushions.

I walked slowly to the table. I didn't dare walk faster than my body could handle on such weak legs. I knew it'd take a bit of time to become stronger.

Elijah brought two bowls of steaming bean soup to the table, right as I sat down, along with a big chunk of toast. My stomach growled at the smell. Taking a little sip of the soup, I found that I liked the flavor. It wasn't too salty like I expected.

I think I had just found one of my favorite foods ever—as long as this man made it, of course.

"I have a list for you to look over tomorrow, once you're more yourself. I don't expect you to be up to reading it and thinking clearly right now with you still recovering. It will include a list of things I expect from you, along with a list of things I would like you to do, but are up to you if you want to do them," Elijah said as we both ate. He ate much faster than I did, as I was trying to not make it look like I was starving, even though I was. I couldn't remember the last time I'd had a decent meal like this.

"I do expect you to be able to communicate with me on any issues or concerns you have. I know most of the things will take time and understanding on my part, but it's all for you. Everything I do is to help you."

"Yes, Sir," I replied, keeping my eyes down. Why would he want to do things for *me*? Wasn't I to do things for *him*?

It was a weird concept, but one I thought sounded nice.

"I also have a list of ways you will be punished if a situation calls for it. I know a little about what you went through. I can guarantee you will be treated with respect in this house and among my family and friends. I do not require any sexual services of any kind from you," he continued. "Emily, my sister-in-law, will be a wonderful person for you to talk to. She has gone through something similar."

"Emily?" I asked, more to myself than the man who sat across from me. I knew a girl named Emily. She was made to watch while I serviced a man because he had given her to Master Galvin as a 'gift'. She had been a blubbering mess the entire time. Just thinking about it made me shudder.

"Do you know her?" Elijah asked, tilting his head to the side as he watched me for any indication.

"I might. . . Sir," I answered, glancing at him. "I didn't know many others there, but a girl named Emily watched when I had to give a man a blow job."

"I see. . . Well, I guess we'll find out in a few days when she comes by," Elijah said, not at all surprised by my words. "Are you done?"

"I guess so, Sir," I answered. I wished for more but was afraid to ask.

"What about some TV then?" he suggested, standing up and taking the bowls and his to the sink.

"If it pleases you, Sir," I replied awkwardly.

"Okay, the 'Sir' thing is going a little too far. You don't have to say it all the time," he sighed, running a hand through his hair.

"Okay . . ."

Shaking his head, he led the way from the kitchen to the living room. The room had black leather furniture and a huge flat screen TV was mounted on the wall.

"Sit down wherever you want," he said.

Elijah sat on the couch, watching and waiting for what I would do. I stood there, not knowing what place to pick. He had said this house would not be anything like I had previously known, but that didn't help knowing where I should sit. I had always been told what to do, down to *how* and *where* to do it.

Undecided and afraid of making a mistake, I made my

way towards Elijah and knelt at his feet. It was the easier choice. Men always liked the girls to be on the floor. I hoped Elijah would be the same. I didn't want to make a mistake and be punished. I really would love to curl up in the big oversized chair with a blanket, or even sit on the couch near him.

He gently ran his fingers along my braided hair. As he moved his hand towards my chin, I couldn't help but lean into his palm and close my eyes. His touch was so much warmer than the men who touched me before now.

It didn't make sense.

"Although I like you kneeling for me, little girl, now really isn't the time," he stated calmly. "How about you come up here and sit beside me." He patted the seat next to him.

I instantly stood, and sat on the couch. My body sank into the cushions; it was almost as soft as the bed. Elijah pulled me by my shoulders so I was leaning against him. I was amazed I wasn't scared. His warmth and old spice smell soothed my nerves. I felt a tingling of déjà vu. I couldn't remember where, but I knew that smell.

Here, wrapped in his arms, I felt protected. It had been too long since I'd felt that way. I knew it wouldn't last, even though I wanted nothing more than that for the rest of my life.

Lost in thought, I jumped in surprise when a cell phone began to ring with some sort of loud song I had never heard before. Elijah rubbed my arm with the end of his fingers to calm me as he turned the TV to mute. I didn't even notice that he'd turned it on.

"Hello," Elijah answered. "How did she find out?" His voice stayed calm, even though his posture stiffened.

"Okay," he continued. "I'll be there in about fifteen minutes, Mom." He hung his phone up, sighing deeply. Turning to me, he said, "I'm sorry, but I have a family issue that needs to be dealt with immediately. You can either stay here and watch TV or go to bed. I shouldn't be too long."

Kissing the top of my head, he then stood up and proceeded to make sure he had his phone before making his way to the entryway, where he had left his shoes and coat. After telling me he would try to not be too long, once again, he closed the door behind him, giving me a look that spoke louder than words: he didn't want to leave me.

I was never a fan of being alone. I'd hated the past few years, even with the lack of hope that I would ever be free. I missed my parents, still not knowing if I would ever see my mom again. I didn't even know if she was still alive, or if she'd tried to look for me. I wasn't sure if I really wanted to see her after everything she'd put me through.

I was afraid of being alone. I had once been locked in a small dark cage that was cold as ice.

Not knowing what to do after he left, as the TV held no interest to me, I walked through the house. I wasn't sure if there were certain rooms I wasn't allowed to enter, so I didn't dare enter any room with a closed door.

Passing the front door for the third time, I decided I would just kneel and wait for Elijah to return. The house felt cold without him, and I didn't know what else to do. There was no way I would be able to sleep if I tried. Kneeling a few feet from the door, I placed my hands behind my back with my head down.

I wasn't used to such quiet. Even while I was kept in that dark cell, I could always hear some sort of noise. Yelling, groaning, crying, and even an occasional gunshot. Being here in this nice warm house, the quiet was so . . .quiet.

"Please, let me go," I sobbed as I was shoved to my knees in front of the man who held my life in his hands.

"Ah, but I can't, my sweets," the man laughed. "I am the man master of this place, and everyone answers to me. I wanted you, therefore I got you."

"Please," I begged. My hands were still tied behind my back. Morgan stood behind me, refusing to answer anything. He was shifty as stood before me.

"You are now mine. You will learn to not speak unless spoken to," the man said as he walked around his desk to where I was kneeling. "I am Master Galvin, and you will give me what I require from scum like you." With that, he snapped his fingers, demanding another man slap my cheek, the noise of skin against skin to echo across the room. I cried out in pain and shock and fell to the side from the force of the blow.

Galvin laughed before pulling me back up to the correct kneeling position. "When I enter a room, you are to be in this position. Eyes down, knees shoulder-width apart, and hands behind your back. If you are not, you will be punished. I will not repeat myself on this rule. Ever."

My breath began to come in heavy pants as the memories crept forth. My palms began to sweat, and I rubbed them on my pant legs. I took a few deep breaths in, hoping that the panic would not get worse.

Please, not now.

I was on my knees with my head pulled back by my hair, my scalp crying out in pain. Master Galvin stood off to the side, watching with a gleeful look. Morgan stood in front of me, one hand in my hair. He had his pants unzipped and down so his hard dick was standing straight up. It was pointing right at me, and the sight of it made me queasy.

"Now, open that mouth of yours. I can't wait to feel the heat around me, sucking me until I shoot my load down your throat." Morgan moaned as he used his other hand to force my mouth open, squeezing my cheeks to the point of pain.

When it was open wide enough, he shoved his cock into my mouth, making me gag as he hit the back of my throat.

"If you bite him, you'll be very sorry," Master Galvin said.

I had learned to stop most of my panic attacks because Master Galvin loved to punish me for them. He'd force one of his men to beat me or use me in a certain way—sometimes both, if he was in a mood.

I could feel the bonds that were almost permanently around my hands those first few months. Of course, if I had only obeyed and not tried to run every chance I got, I may have had a few less bruises. The men were not gentle. I don't think they even knew what the word meant.

Apparently, I didn't do a good enough job giving Morgan my first blow job, because after his grunting and groaning and shooting his cum down my throat, I was shoved backward, barely catching myself on my tied hands.

"You're worthless!" Morgan snarled as he tucked himself back into his pants. "Your mother was better."

He then kicked me in the stomach, knocking the breath out of me.

That wasn't the last time. I had been forced to practice on the men for days on end, until it was what they deemed to be good enough. My jaw hurt constantly, making me unable to eat much of anything for days.

Rocking back and forth, my heart felt like it was going to beat out of my chest. I covered my face with my hands, folding my body in two.

The front door opened, letting in a wave of cold air.

The first time I panicked was right after I was released from the burning ropes and shut in what I would be calling my home for years to come. I was worried about my mom, worried about finding a way out of hell. I refused to let those men have their way with my body without a fight. And I would fight. I would fight till my last dying breath. But it didn't do any good. The men always won.

"Oh honey," said a female voice quietly nearby. The presence of another slowly brought me back to the present. "Come on. Up you get."

The woman gently pulled me up and I didn't fight. I was tired, sore, and scared. All my fight had long since been beaten out of me.

What was the point in fighting anymore?

I removed my hands from my face and wrapped them around my middle. I could feel my ribs cry out in pain from the pressure and remembrance of old breaks that had never healed quite right, but it was better than the blackness that wanted to take over. I was led to the couch where the lady sat down and pulled my head to her lap. My tears continued. She unbraided my hair and began to run her fingers through my black locks.

Surprisingly, my breaths began to even out and my tears slowed. My heartbeat slowly calmed and I stared blankly at the table in front of me.

I jerked when a blanket was laid over my body, and that's when I noticed I was shaking. My legs were pulled up to my chest and my teeth were chattering. My entire body was shivering from the inside out.

"It's okay," the female said, not stopping her fingers. "It's only Zack. You're freezing."

"S . . . s. . . sorry," I stuttered out.

"Don't worry, Dawn," she shushed, her voice soothing like a mother's voice.

"Emily, baby? I'm gonna give Elijah a call," said the man named Zack quietly from where he stood behind the couch. I hoped he wouldn't get any closer to me.

I couldn't help but compare his voice to Sir's. It was soft and soothing, just like Elijah's.

"Okay," she replied, just as quiet. "Why were you scared, Dawn?" she asked me.

"Too quiet," I whispered as my body began to warm. "No one here."

"The TV was on," she pointed out. "But I can understand. I had a few panic attacks the first few weeks after I was rescued, and I was there for less than a week. I couldn't stand to be touched, or to be alone with just my thoughts. I hated it.

Of course, my life wasn't much better before my boyfriend sold me to Galvin and his crew."

"I saved her, though," Zack said as he plopped into the chair closest to us. "Took me two months before I could touch her, and six months to earn her trust, but we've made it this far."

"And my love," the female—Emily—whispered with a smile.

"That, too," Zack laughed awkwardly. "Anyway, Elijah should be back within the hour. We should have been here before he left. I'm sorry we weren't."

After a few minutes of silence between the three of us, Zack grabbed the remote from the coffee table where Elijah had left it and changed the channel. I closed my eyes, too tired to keep them open any longer as I enjoyed the soothing feeling of Emily playing with my hair.

CHAPTER 6

ELIJAH

I didn't want to leave Dawn, but when my mother called in near panic, I didn't have much choice. I figured she would be okay by herself for a few minutes and I would call my brother once I was in the car.

Once in the car and backing out of my spot, I called my brother. He owed me enough favors, so he certainly could do me one now.

"What's up bro?" he answered on the fourth ring. He was always the happy person out of the two of us. I just went with the flow and got the job done, whatever it was.

"Really? Do you have to shout?" I asked. "Can you do me a huge favor?"

"Sure," he answered. I could mentally see him shrug.

"Can you go check on Dawn? And take Emily with you. Mom called and said Joan showed up and wants some answers," I said.

"Yep. I've been waiting to see little Dawn again," he replied.

I knew he'd be disappointed, since the girl he remembered was not the same in any way—not after what she'd been through.

"Just be careful, please. She's not like you remember," I warned, hoping that he wouldn't be hurt.

"Yeah, I gotcha, Elijah," he said sadly.

I had been scared out of my mind a few weeks ago when I had left her with my mom and she told me Dawn was coughing, and could hardly move through the pain. I'd called my dad instantly. That week was the longest of my life. I was by her side as much as I possibly could be.

I grew up with a bright-eyed girl who wasn't afraid of anything and always spoke her mind. We were close as we possibly could be for our ages—like cousins. Dawn was nine years younger than me, like a little sister who drove me nuts most of the time. She'd follow me everywhere, asking me question after question or just talking non-stop. My brother, who was five years older than me, constantly made fun of me because I had a shadow who thought I'd hung the moon.

The get-togethers grew farther apart as we grew older. Mom began to work more hours at the homeless shelters around town, and my brother and I began to get into sports and more involved in school.

When we heard about Quentin's death, we dropped everything to help Dawn and Joan, even offering them the space above the garage at my parents' home. Joan declined, even though my parents knew that where they lived wasn't the best place.

I went off to college and entered the FBI program, following Zack a year later. Determination and the lack of family ties of a wife or children was the main reason we gained positions so quickly. After getting into the FBI, Zack was able to dig up the case on Dawn. At that time, they didn't have much information, or the interview transcripts in the file. He found out they were ruling the case as a runaway.

I didn't think it was the normal runaway: I had seen a fair share of them, but I couldn't say anything, since we were not allowed to be on the case.

When my mother called, saying Joan knew Dawn had been found and wanted answers, I knew I would have to come up with something to tide her over. I wanted to know who told her.

Looking at the house with almost all the lights on downstairs, I took a deep breath before I made my way out of the car.

"Elijah," my mother said, relieved. She pulled me into a tight hug as I closed the front door behind me. "I tried to get her to understand that I didn't know anything," she whispered near my ear.

"I'll handle it," I stated before my mom released me.

"Good to see you, Mrs. Ellis," I greeted as I entered the living room. My voice was monotonous as I addressed the woman before me. The living room was laid out in a similar way as my own but in lighter colors. The walls were painted a dark blue color, making the oak and white furniture stand out more.

The woman sat on the white couch, clutching a tissue in her hands. Her dull green eyes were red and puffy from crying. Her face had more wrinkles around her eyes and mouth. As a teenager, I always thought Joan was in her twenties instead of late thirties. Her light blond hair had a few gray strands now as it was pulled into a sloppy ponytail. She looked old—and that was putting it nicely.

She was a drug addict, and looked as though she still used drugs. My best guess was meth and black market pills.

"So, is it true? Has my baby has been found?" she cried. Her eyes pleaded for me to give her the information she wanted so desperately.

"I'm not at liberty to say," I said, stuffing my hands in my pockets and leaning against the door frame between the

43

living room and entryway. "You know I'm not on that case for personal reasons. Who told you, anyhow?"

"Morgan knows a guy who told him," she answered. I knew it was going to be that deadbeat. "You dug up information once before. You can do it again. I need to know where my daughter is. Please," she begged, leaning forward, still clutching the white tissue.

I could understand her need for answers, but with it still being an open investigation, and Dawn being eighteen, Joan was not meant to know anything. She still wasn't ruled out as a suspect in the case.

"I'm not on the case, so I don't have any information. My guess is she's been put into witness protection because her kidnappers have not been identified."

"Can't you get Zack to ask around and get some information? Or have him hack into the system to find out where she is?"

"No, I can't. He nearly lost his badge the last time; he won't risk it again."

"But I want to see my daughter!" she wailed. "I'll do anything to just see her."

"I know you do, and I'm sure you will. You just have to be patient," my father said calmly as he walked into the room, patting me on my shoulder on his way past me. He was still in his blue work scrubs, a clear sign he hadn't taken the time to shower before leaving the hospital after his shift.

"I won't stop until I see her," Joan said, her voice turning cold.

"You are just going to have to wait," I said. There was nothing I'd do right now. Not willinging anyhow.

My phone began to ring, and I excused myself to answer it in another room. I was relieved to get away from the grieving woman. Why hadn't my mother called Zack instead?

"Yeah?" I answered, seeing it was my brother calling.

"Yo, Eli man," he greeted me.

"I'm busy, Zack," I sighed, rubbing at my eyes with my free hand.

"What were you thinking, leaving her alone? It was only fifteen minutes, but she was totally lost in her mind," he nearly shouted.

"I thought she'd be okay. I expected her to just go to bed," I stated, rubbing a hand down my face.

"Well, she didn't. She was kneeling by the door on her knees waiting for you to return. She was obviously in full-out panic mode. You should have called me before you left the house," he said, lowering his voice as anger dissolved from his voice. "You're lucky Emily came with me, Elijah. I have no idea how to handle women; she was bad enough."

"Yeah," I replied, at a loss for words. "Did she say anything?"

"No," he laughed sadly. "She panicked even more when I tried to get near her. Took my Emily a good ten minutes to get her to calm down enough to move off the floor.

"Tell her thank you for me," I said. I wanted to punch myself for being so stupid, but what was done was done. There was nothing I could do about it now.

"You can tell her yourself," he replied. "And are you sure this girl is our Dawn? She's so . . . sad…"

"Yeah, it is. The DNA test results are a match," I answered quietly, so I wouldn't have to worry about being overheard. "I hope to be back once I can get Joan calmed down."

"Alright bro, bye." Zack ended the call.

Walking back to the living room, I found my parents sitting on the loveseat and Joan sitting in the same spot she was before. She held her hands in her lap and kept sniffling. She looked up when I re-entered the room.

"So, can you find some info on my baby? Please, Elijah?" she begged with sad eyes. I was good at reading people, and this woman here was certainly putting on a good act.

"I'll see what I can do. I won't be able to find her location, but I can hopefully get something on how she is doing. Now, if you'll excuse me, I have to get back to my guest," I said, hoping to pacify her for the time being.

I bid my parents goodbye and dad walked out with me. The sun had long sat on the horizon, casting long, dark shadows around the yard.

"Thank you, son," he stated once we were outside. "Joslyn couldn't figure out a way to get her to calm down, and there was an emergency at the hospital so I couldn't leave.

"Thank you, Dad," I said, before I made my way to the car. I shot Zack a text, letting him know I was on my way home.

I tried to be quiet so I wouldn't wake Dawn if she was asleep by chance when I got back. I may have even exceeded the speed limit to get there faster because I was so worried about her.

Reaching the living room of my house, the scene made my heart break once again. Dawn was the only girl who could ever cause me this type of weakness. My girl was lying on the couch with her head in Emily's lap. She had an afghan covering her as she lay there. Occasionally, I could see tremors go through her body. She looked worse than when I'd left her.

What had I done?

Zack sat in the chair closest to the door. He was looking at the TV but I could tell from his face that he was worried. So was I. I had no idea what to do to make Dawn happy and healthy again. She wasn't a simple fun-loving girl anymore.

I patted him on his upper arm, drawing his attention away from wherever his mind was. I walked to the couch, crouching down next to Dawn right as her green eyes slowly opened into a dazed look. They were filled with nothing, almost completely blank. It was as if she had no reason to live—nothing to fight for any longer.

"Hey there," I said to her, letting my southern drawl break

BROKEN REVIVAL

through. "You ready to go to bed so we can let Zack and Emily go home?" I wanted her to hear my accent.

Over the past five years, I had train myself to speak in a region neutral accent. However, Dawn would only remember me with that southern twang from when I was younger. Whether she did or not, I hoped the accent would comfort her.

Instead of answering me, she only blinked. I yearned to see the young, bright-eyed girl reappear.

"I'm sorry for putting you in a position where you were left alone and afraid. I didn't think clearly," I said, keeping my hands to myself, even though I wanted to pull her into a tight hug and never let her go.

"She'll be okay," Emily whispered. "Give her some time and show her you're not mad."

"Oh, I can't be mad; it was my fault," I said, running the back of my hand down the side of her face. She closed her eyes at the contact and cradled her face in my hand, seeming to want to soak up any affection she could from me. "Now let's get you to bed, Dawn."

I knew without a doubt that Zak's Emily was the Emily in the cages with my girl for a short time. Surely she wouldn't have taken so easily to anyone she didn't know?

Once I had her in my arms, she buried her head into my shoulder and neck as her small hands clenched my shirt like her life depended on it.

I vaguely heard my brother and soon to be sister-in-law make their way out of the house. I carried Dawn up to my bedroom, knowing she wasn't going to want to be in her own bed by herself. Plus, I wanted to hold her until she felt safe. I attempted to lay her on my bed, but she clung to me tighter, if that were possible.

"I won't leave you. I'm just laying you down on the bed," I said gently.

"Stay?" she cried, glancing up through her long eyelashes,

spiked with tears. More tears were gathering in her eyes as she looked at me.

"Of course," I answered, smiling tenderly at her.

She slowly released her hold on me so I could lay her down. I watched her as she began to stiffen with wide eyes as she watched me. I took my shoes off and sat my phone and keys on the side table. My bedroom was set up similarly to hers. The only difference was instead of the light brown colors, my room was bathed in grays, blacks and whites, and I had a king size bed.

Once I was in bed, laying on my back with only the glow of a small lamp to fend off the darkness, I pulled the frightened girl closer to me, where she instantly curled into my side. I had shed my shirt, so her soft warmth soaked into me even more.

CHAPTER 7

DAWN

*T*he thumping of a heart reached my senses as I slowly woke up. My cheek was pressed against Elijah's chest that, at some point during the night, I had decided to use as a pillow. His breathing was slow and even as he slept. I think that was one of the most peaceful night's sleep I'd had in years. I was warm, comfy, and surprisingly refreshed. I almost didn't want to wake up and face reality.

When I was rented, the rooms that did have beds were not used as a place to sleep. If I was lucky, the men would pass out after getting their fill and I would lie there, unable to sleep as the sounds around me would continue. It was almost worse than the dark and quiet when I was locked away. I never knew what might happen to me if I fell asleep.

I had no idea how long I dozed, lying in Emily's lap, before Sir came back. I couldn't recall what was said between the three, but Elijah seemed worried, or maybe angry, when I saw him in front of me. Despite whatever he felt, he picked me up and carried me up to his room, where I expected him to either leave me or have his way with me like Morgan and the other handlers always did. I felt so weak and tired.

I had asked, almost cried, even, for the man to stay, even with the risk of him hurting me in any way, just so I didn't have to be left alone. I wasn't able to deal with the panic-filled memories I knew would take over if I was left alone again. He surprised me by getting into bed and pulling me to his side, instantly soothing my nerves. It hadn't taken me long to fall asleep wrapped in his embrace.

I hid my feelings for so long, refusing to allow myself to feel anything at all, knowing it would hurt worse. I hated it, but if I wanted to survive those cages, I couldn't do anything differently.

Glancing down, I saw the comforter tented a little at Sir's crotch. Feeling a little brave, I wanted to show the man I was thankful for everything so far: warm clothes, a bed where I could sleep, and good food. I gently and slowly moved my right hand down to his dick. Sometime during the night, he'd shed his pants and only had thin boxers on, where his tip was poking out.

Slowly, as not to awaken him, I pushed the material down around him. I then made my way down his body so I could use my mouth on him, leaving the covers over my head. The warm, stifling air was nothing I couldn't handle. He smelled so good, a mix between some kind of cologne, soap, and the musky scent of a clean man. Normally, the men I serviced were filthy, grime embedded in their skin, the scent of stale sex and body odor rancid. Sir was different.

Wanting to surprise him, I sucked on the tip before taking him fully in my mouth. He was very hard and thick by then. I sucked on him, swiping my tongue underneath on the vein, making him arch up and slide down my throat some.

Pulling back a little, I tenderly nibbled him before taking him in my mouth again, making him moan deep in his chest. I smiled, because for once in my crappy life, I was happy and content. I hummed against his member, and his hand grabbed my head, fisting my hair but not too hard. Most men never cared if they hurt me, and I had grown used to the pain—almost craved it, some days.

"Oh, fuck," Elijah moaned as I released him and sucked on the mushroom head of his cock again. He quickly used his other hand to pull back the blanket. I looked up at him through my eyelashes. I could tell he wasn't sure what to do: demand I stop or let me continue. His face was controlled, but his eyes shone with pure want and lust.

Quickly before he could decide, I took him all the way in my mouth. He was so long he hit the back of my throat. I moaned around him, liking the hardness of him. I had never before liked to give blow jobs, but I would do it every day for this man, if he'd allow me.

Elijah's hand tangled in my hair, giving into my ministrations and letting his bright blue eyes close as he took deep breaths. I moved my hand into his boxers and played with his balls, rolling them softly. He muttered a soft "fuck" as he exploded down my throat. I gladly swallowed everything he gave me.

Pulling me off him, he was breathless but spoke with authority. "Come back up here." I obeyed, hoping I wouldn't be in trouble.

"Not that I can complain to such a great wake up call, but you didn't need to do that," he said once I was back up near the pillows. "But, that was the best blow job ever."

"I've had a lot of practice, Sir," I whispered, near tears. Was I in trouble?

"Oh, sweet girl, you are going to be hard to resist," he mumbled as he kissed the top of my head. "I think you should get ready for breakfast. We have a few things we need to talk about—like how I expect you to act around here."

"Yes, Sir," I said, not knowing how to respond otherwise.

Slowly making my way off the bed and to my room across

the hall, my fears grew. I didn't know what would happen. Would I be punished? Would he make me go back to Master Galvin and Morgan?

After taking a shower and getting dressed, I made my way down to the kitchen. My nerves were finally calm, knowing that if I had survived this long, I could make it through whatever he had in store for me.

On the table sat two steaming bowls of oatmeal. He already sat with a bowl, watching me as I entered and took my seat. He didn't say anything as I began to eat.

"Why were you in such a panic last night?" he began, his voice soft.

I remained quiet, pretty sure he already knew why, and not wanting to voice my fears. I wasn't a child and shouldn't be afraid to be left alone for any length of time. Galvin enjoyed punishing me for little things, no matter what it was. I hoped Sir wouldn't do that to me.

"Answer me, Dawn, and please be truthful," Elijah said as he stared at me with those brown eyes. "What made you so afraid? Was it because you were alone, or because you didn't know what to do?"

"Both, Sir," I whispered, trying to look anywhere but at the man across from me. I didn't want him to see how upset I was. I could hardly see through my tears.

"Dawn," he warned, his voice hardening.

"I don't like to be alone, Sir. Master Galvin liked to leave me alone for days at a time. He would punish me with the dark and being alone. No one would come and feed me." I spoke quietly, feeling ashamed of myself for my weakness. "And . . . I didn't know what you wanted me to do, Sir. Morgan and the other men would tell me exactly what they wanted me to do, all of the time, unless they were trying to trick me." By now, tears slowly fell down my cheeks.

"I'm sorry I wasn't clear about what you could have done. I should have waited until Zack arrived before I left you here to your own devices," Elijah said. "I know I should have gone over the rules before now, but you were sick and I didn't feel like you would be able to stay coherent long enough for me to do so."

I looked up at him, and I could see that he truly was sorry. I wasn't sure how to take that, as no one had ever apologized to me when I was with Master Galvin.

"So, once you're finished eating, you are to meet me in my office and we will go over the rules and punishments of this house. We will both agree on these rules and consequences together. I want you to be honest with me the entire time. Understood?" his eyes locked on my own.

"Yes, Sir," I said. I was scared, but I also felt better, knowing I would be able to have some sort of guidelines to follow so I could do my best to not be punished.

Elijah took care of his bowl before leaving me to finish my own food. After a few minutes and not able to stomach anymore, I took care of my own bowl, not caring if I'd get in trouble for wasting the food.

By the time I made it to Elijah's office, I could feel the onset of panic again. I really had no idea why I was so scared. Either Elijah didn't know I was on the verge, or chose to ignore it, as he simply smiled at me when I entered quietly. He told me to take a seat in the brown leather chair he'd moved beside his desk.

His office was off the living room, with a set of white French doors; his space was clean and colored like the rest of the house. Elijah sat in a fancy office chair.

"Before we begin, I want you to know that you will not be in any trouble at all while we discuss things. I want you to be open with me."

I simply nodded my head. I tried to stop my hands from shaking by folding them in my lap.

"First, I will start with what I would like you to do, since my hours at work are usually long, both day and night. I would like my laundry to be washed, folded and put away, along with yours, in a timely manner. I try to put all my dirty clothes in the hamper in the bathroom, but sometimes my clothes end up around the bedroom. Later, I will let you explore the house and figure out where everything is.

"You don't have to do any of it, if you don't want, of course. I just think that if you have something to do to keep your mind and body busy, then you won't get lost in your mind and have as many panic attacks." He paused then, waiting for me to respond.

"I don't mind cleaning," I said after a moment. "If it's what you want me to do . . ."

"It's not what I want," he was quick to assure me. "It's what *you* want, Dawn. You never have to do anything, never lift a finger, or even see me, if you don't want to."

He paused, letting that sink in before continuing.

"I would like my bed sheets washed and changed at least once a week. I don't expect the entire house to be spotlessly clean, but I do want my bathroom, the bathroom down here, the living room, this office and the kitchen to be cleaned, and kept clean as much as possible. I have guests who like to pop in without calling. It's important that these more public rooms stay as clean as you can keep them.

"On the nights I am home, I would enjoy having a nice warm meal made for both of us to eat together. I will be sure to let you know ahead of time, so you can get the meal prepared. Joslyn and Emily will be more than happy to help you if you need anything, of course. If you are hungry, at any time, you are free to eat or drink anything you want in this house.

"I also expect you to be polite to me and to anyone who comes in this house, and when you are out with me or my family. Rudeness will not be tolerated. Anything I say to anyone is never to be repeated to anyone ever.

"If you have any questions or concerns, you must always

come to me at any time to ask me what to do. If I'm not here, you can ask Kaleb or Zak. They are the two exceptions to the not repeating anything rule. I don't expect anything sexual from you in any way. I don't want a repeat of this morning until I know you are stable mentally and physically. This is very important, Dawn."

"But you liked the blow job," I blurted out. I quickly covered my mouth with my hands as my eyes widened. *Did I just say that out loud?*

"Yes, yes I did," he laughed, leaning back in his chair. His laugh was soft but full of humor. "I know you are used to being used and abused in many ways, but you will never be treated like that here. I will get you whatever you need, any desire or want, within reason. I will never take advantage of you like that. I will never expect you to provide me, or anyone else, with sex.

"You will be treated with respect—like a person. You are *not* a slave in this house, and I know my mother already considers you family. It is my job to make sure you are happy here. But I don't require that type of service from you. We not in the type of relationship to take that step yet. Maybe someday we will, but not for some time.

"Do you know anything about BDSM?" he asked, leaning forward again. He gently took my hands and held them in his bigger hands.

"No, not really, Sir," I answered.

"I am a Dom—a Dominant. I like to control everything, especially sexually," he said, making sure I was paying attention. "I will try my best to not overwhelm you, not with your history, but I do like order, and insist on having your respect. I will only give out punishments when—and that is a big *when*—we play in a scene. I will never just punish you because you didn't do what I wanted. That's not how this relationship works; no relationship, actually.

"Some Doms like to use canes and whips, but I personally

do not like them, therefore I will never use one as a tool of punishment on you.

"If you disobey by being disrespectful, you will be given a warning to remind you. The second time, you will get a punishment, which most likely will be a simple spanking or a privilege taken away, such as TV, or reading a book."

So, all he wanted was respect from me?

That didn't seem bad at all, not when compared to what I was used to. More often than not, I was kicked or beaten and left breathless until one of the men would roughly pick me up or drag me back to my cage. Of course, I didn't want to push this man in any way, so I would make sure to do everything he wanted me to do, as best as I could.

"I can be good, Sir," I said, finally able to breathe easily again.

"I know you can," he smiled tenderly. "Now, do you have any questions for me?"

"No, Sir," I said, shaking my head.

"Okay. In your free time," he went on. "You are can read a book, watch TV, do puzzles, or anything else you may want to try. I will have Joslyn bring some books over that may be more of an interest to you than what I have here, since they're mostly history and a few BDSM handbooks, which you may become interested in later.

"The reason I became a FBI agent was because I wanted to put a stop to what has happened to you." I gasped, shocked. I hadn't expected him to work for that type of work. "And so it won't happen to others. It's not the way of life anyone should be forced to live. That's why I require my real last name not be said while in the company of certain people, and why you can't be allowed to repeat things you hear," he explained. "But when it is just the two of us, you are free to ask me anything you'd like. I will always try to give you an answer."

"Okay, Sir," I said.

"For now, how about you find a book to read while I finish

typing up some reports? Then, we can explore the house," he said, standing up and patting me on my knee. I stood quickly when he did, so he moved the chair back by the others.

With wide eyes, I slowly made my way to the bookshelf, not really knowing what to read. I hadn't been allowed to for over five years. I picked a random book, knowing I wouldn't be reading much of it since I knew I needed to be alert and aware of my surroundings. It was so easy to relax here. I needed to be careful so I followed his rules and didn't break any of them accidently.

Getting comfy on the window seat, I opened the book and attempted to read. The first few pages didn't hold my attention. The clicking of the keyboard as Elijah typed was soothing in the quietness. Before I knew it, I leaned my head against the window and I fell asleep, not fearing any painful surprises.

CHAPTER 8

ELIJAH

My talk with Dawn went much smoother than I thought it would. I wasn't sure how she would take all the information I had given her, and hoped she'd come talk to me about any worries or questions. I was prepared for her to panic again, since I could tell the fear was just beneath the calm façade she was trying so desperately to keep.

Most of my new subs never questioned the rules that would be printed on paper in a normal Dom/sub contract. They knew what to expect. They understood the power exchanges between a Dominant and his submissive. They already knew they had all the control in the relationship. With Dawn, I had to go about it differently. She would agree to anything to please me, even if she didn't want to do it—that was how she was trained. That's why I made sure that she knew she could have a say; something I'd have to remind her about frequently.

It was going to take time for her to decide if she really

wanted that type of relationship. I couldn't be sure if she did want, or even if she understood, that lifestyle. I was not going to push it on her, knowing she'd do whatever I wanted. It would be my mission to help her decide if she enjoyed being a sub or not—all of which would take time. I would be okay with Dawn being whatever she desired. If she was into the vanilla lifestyle, being a Domme, or even a mix of everything, I'd be okay with that.

The morning wake-up call had been unexpected. I'd had a lot of blow jobs in my lifetime, but none had been as good as that. I don't know if it was the innocence of her youth, or just the connection I had with her when we were younger. Then, she used her mouth on my dick, and I had never come so hard from a simple blow job before.

Watching Emily and Zack, I had some indication as to how my girl would react to certain situations. I knew there was a low possibility she would try to test my boundaries, but hopefully not for a very long time with what she'd been through. That's why I gave her my idea of a punishment, so she wouldn't worry about what would happen. I'd hate to see her go into panic mode because I wasn't clear enough on what might happen punishment-wise in this house. I had to start somewhere to get her to see that I wouldn't push her around just because I was a man.

I also wanted to see how Dawn would cope with everything I had explained. I couldn't wait to see how she would test the boundaries once she was fully healed, mentally and physically.

I worried she'd not take to any of it, but I was willing to compromise. I'd do anything to help Dawn understand what a Dom/sub relationship was like, along with helping her learn that it was different than a Master/slave relationship. It would be a lot of work, but something that needed to be done. She needed to know that there were other ways to live. Fuck, I'd even show her what a normal, vanilla relationship—

minus the sex part—was like. That would be the best place to start.

I cared deeply for Dawn, and always would. When she used to follow me around, she would tell everyone that she was going to marry me someday.

The day she was born, she owned my heart. It certainly wasn't any different now.

After going over the simple rules and expectations, I had Dawn pick out a book. It didn't take long for her to grab one and curl up in the window seat. No submissive had ever sat there before; they would always kneel by me or sit in one of the chairs if I allowed them.

I opened my computer and answered a few emails from work that demanded my attention. When I looked over at Dawn, I could tell she had no interest in the history novel she had picked. I quickly sent a text to Joslyn, asking her to find something that Dawn might like to read better than what I had to offer here.

It was only a few minutes later when I looked over at her again, I saw that she was fast asleep. Leaning back in my chair, I just watched her. Her face was relaxed, her long, slightly wavy hair falling around her shoulders. She looked so young and innocent.

I could remember the first time I ever laid eyes on Dawn. She was a week old and wrapped up in a soft blanket. Zack, who was more interested in his new toy, had wanted nothing to do with the new baby. I had been bugging my mother non-stop, wanting to meet the new little one who would become my best friend. It had been a long week before I finally got to see her. She was the most adorable little thing ever.

I couldn't contain the huge smile that took over my face as I held the new baby. Dawn had just opened her big eyes and intently stared at me.

I instantly fell in love with her, and I'm sure my mother took a picture to capture the moment.

"I'm going to marry you one day, Dawn Elizabeth," I had declared, knowing I would do anything and everything in my power to make sure this baby would never know pain. I swore in my head I would always protect her.

Remembering my failed promise, I was consumed by guilt. I had failed her. I'm not sure when I had begun to slip away from her; somewhere just before Quentin's death. I wasn't there for her when she needed me the most.

I let my head fall backward, taking deep breaths. I was more determined than ever to make sure Dawn would be happy and to keep her safe. I would do anything in my power to do so.

I became interested in it all while in college but always had the characteristics since I was a young kid. Control over things helped me cope with the stresses of life. It helped when Dawn disappeared, even though it tore my world apart.

Hearing about her disappearance tore me up inside. It ran through my blood, never leaving me. I wanted to cry, but only boys cried. I was a man, and had no time for such emotions. I constantly wanted to throw something, punch something—or some*one*…anything to make the feelings go away.

The ringing of my cell phone jolted me back to reality. The sound echoed in the room, making Dawn to jump, dropping the book to the floor.

"Hello?" I answered, not looking at who was calling as I watched the embarrassed girl pick up the book before rubbing the sleep from her eyes.

"Elijah," greeted my boss, knowing not to call me by my last name like he would normally do at work.

"Kaleb," I replied, surprised he was calling. He'd hadn't for a while, and not while on this case, due to the fact that the phone line might be monitored. I'd called him a few times from the untraceable secure cellphone I kept hidden

"I'll be by in about an hour. There're some things I need to get you up to date on."

"Alright, see you then," I said before he hung up.

Curious, but not too concerned, I turned to the girl in the window. She blushed at my gaze and I simply smiled. "How about that tour?" I asked, hoping my voice stayed calm.

She nodded before getting to her feet and making her way to where I still sat in the chair.

After stopping at the bathroom, since I was sure she must need to take a moment but wouldn't dare voice the need, I took her through the house. I led her to the laundry/mud room at the back through the kitchen.

The laundry room held shelving and a folding area along one wall, while along the wall across from that sat the LG washer and dryer. I showed her how they worked, and the settings I wanted her to use. I opened each cupboard, showing Dawn where the cleaning supplies were.

I showed her where all the dishes and food were in the kitchen and the pantry, so she could find things when she cooked.

"I don't expect you to remember where everything is. It took me months, and I still forget where my mother put everything," I said, easing the worry etched onto her face.

I then led her upstairs, pointing out the two spare bedrooms that would need to be touched up sometime in the next week or two.

I pointed out the door at the end of the hall that led to the attic. "That door is to stay closed, and I highly advise you to not venture up there. Most of it is just storage and doesn't need to be dusted, but it's also my playroom. Kaleb and I have the only keys. I am the only one who will clean in that room, and it doesn't get used all too often."

"Okay, Sir," she said. She most likely didn't even know what a playroom was, so I wasn't worried.

I knew it wouldn't take her much to keep the house clean. I had Emily come by once every two weeks to do it for me. It gave her something to do, and helped her get out of the house without Zack. I normally did my own laundry.

"In a few minutes, I have a friend stopping by. I want you to be in the office while we talk. You can do anything: reading, watching outside, dusting even, if you wanted—as long as I can see you," I said as I gently lifted her chin to meet my eyes. Her green eyes shone just a tad brighter and clearer. I hoped it meant she was starting to feel better.

"Yes, Sir," she said. Even though she still guarded her emotions, I knew she was feeling better about knowing what I expected from her. Truthfully, I didn't want to have her do anything. I would gladly let her lie around all day if she wanted.

I did need to get more information from her, sooner rather than later, about what she'd gone through. Maybe Kaleb could get something out of her for me.

Kaleb was a few years older than me, but he was the chief and my boss, before being my friend. He was a pretty laid-back guy unless in Dom mode. I was thankful to him for introducing me into the life I now knew. I met him at an open night at a highly sought out club. He showed me the new lifestyle, teaching me how to read subs and Doms alike.

Of course, I had to learn to be a sub before being a Dom. I hated subbing, giving into another as they controlled my body, my pain, and my pleasure. But I did so willingly with Kaleb, allowing him to take control because I trusted him. That was, until he found the girl with whom he wanted to share his life. That was when he guided me into being a Dom, picking women for me who had been subs for years.

Dawn was the first woman I was interested in who had no idea what kind of life I had lived, let alone who employed me. Zack knew of my sex life, as I had to explain a few things for him to help Emily. They both now play around with a few scenes and a few toys but I didn't want to know the details.

When I heard a knock on my front door, I looked at Dawn,

nodded towards my office area, and she walked away from me into the office with a worried look on her face. She really had no reason to, but I knew she didn't know that.

"Kaleb!" I greeted him, opening the door. His face was the first thing I saw. It was still tanned like he was always out in the sun, but I knew he was hardly outside anymore with the demands of this case—along with others. His bright gray eyes were the same as always, just a tad bit tired.

"Elijah," he smiled in return, stepping into to the house. He wore blue jeans and a button-up checkered shirt with cowboy boots. He always wore western style clothing, showing off his heritage as much as possible. "How are you today?"

"Not too bad," he replied. He immediately invaded my personal space and wrapped his long arms round me, giving me a hard hug that made me completely relax. Then, he started walking towards my office, being the type to always get to the point first. He was a dominant alpha male in all areas of his life, and power just seemed to ooze from him in waves.

I followed him to my office. He sat in the middle chair and I went to my desk. Seeing Dawn had already gotten three bottles of water out, I threw one to Kaleb before acknowledging her. She was kneeling beside my chair with her head down and hands in her lap. Her knees were shoulder width apart, her hair hiding her face as I had yet to braid it for her. My heart soared, seeing her there, knowing she willingly chose to submit, but then it plummeted as I remembered why she was here and what might happen with Kaleb.

"Have a seat on a chair, Dawn," I said softly. There was no way I was going to have her stay kneeling on the carpet.

She stood and took a seat by the window, but kept her head down. I sighed, knowing my work was cut out for me with her.

"We have a rat, of which I'm sure you are well aware,"

Kaleb began in his lighter voice, like it was an everyday conversation. I could read the worry in his eyes. "I'm fairly certain who it is."

"Mike Hughes?" I asked, handing Dawn a bottle of water after opening it for her.

"Yep," he stated, leaning back in his chair. "We can't draw any attention to it, though. He's been digging and not cleaning up his tracks. He's left files open on computers; I know he's working on trying to frame you. I just don't know why."

"Revenge? I busted his brother not too long ago. I know Mike has never exactly liked me for that reason," I responded thoughtfully.

"Possibly," Kaleb said. "He may be trying to cover something up, and trying to pin it on you and make our case fall apart somehow."

"No one knows my rule but you and Zack. I've made sure nothing I do can be traced back in any way, shape or form to the real me. I know I'm treading a pretty fine line, pretending to be a man who is intent on becoming a dirty agent for the money I can get."

"You do know what will happen before the case is brought to a close, right?" he asked with a hint of worry.

"Yes. I have a wonderful lawyer on standby, and I won't be held for more than a week at the most, or charged with anything. I will have to act as if it's the end of the world so the people we are trying to bring down will think I was busted. But of course, you'll come to get me out and show proof to the officer in charge of who and what I really am doing." I answered. "Of course, I may not have to be arrested and questioned if the suspects are caught before the planned time."

"What is your plan for the girl?" Kaleb asked, wanting to make sure Dawn knew what to expect when the time came.

"You already know," I said. "Dawn will be going with

either you or Zack; the least likely places someone would look for her." Of course, she looked at me when I said her name and I couldn't help but gently smile at her, letting her know everything was okay.

"Now, let me meet this girl who's kept you home from your job for so long," he grinned.

"Come, Dawn," I said. She stood, her body stiff. I could see the fear in her eyes as she walked to me. How many men had used her? What had they done to make her so pliable?

She relaxed a little as I took her hand, which in turn made me feel better. I led her around the desk and stopped in front of Kaleb. Lifting her head up with my finger under her chin, and then stroking her cheek, I smiled, showing no harm would come to her.

"Dawn, this is Kaleb." She briefly looked him over before lowering her eyes as soon as I dropped my hand from her face. "There will come a time when you might have to go with him, but only as a means to keep you safe. He won't ever hurt you in any way. His wife would never allow him to do so."

"Yeah, Kelly would have my nuts on a platter," Kaleb joked. "How old are you, anyway?"

"Nineteen, I think, Sir," she answered quietly, squeezing my hand tightly.

"You look younger," he said, tilting his head as he looked at her a bit closer.

I moved towards the chair on his right, with Dawn following. Once I sat down, I pulled her so she could sit in my lap. She scrunched up as much as she could, with her head between my neck and shoulder and her legs laying over the armrest. Her face was towards Kaleb, even though her hair was mostly covering the view.

"Yes. She was only fourteen when she was taken. With the lack of food, she will look younger. Once we get her back to good and healthy eating habits, she should gain some weight. Her mother didn't look her age at all until recently."

"You grew up together, correct?"

"We did. I don't know how much she remembers from her childhood," I answered, squeezing her hand in reassurance.

"I'm sure Joslyn has stories," he winked at me. "And I bet you were a cute baby and handsome little man. Kaleb would never be unfaithful to Kelly, but he was just naturally a flirt. He gave me a wink and turned his attention to Dawn.

"Dawn, can I ask you a few questions?" he said quietly but with authority. He became the Dom and special agent in charge that I knew so well after over six years. He kept his voice calm, but the authority and respect that he demanded just by his presence were there.

Dawn only nodded, burying herself more into me, if it were possible. I hoped she might be beginning to see me as her safe place.

CHAPTER 9

DAWN

Truthfully, I never wanted to leave Elijah's lap. I felt like I belonged there. My head fit perfectly against his neck, where I could breathe in his scent. I wasn't sure about his friend, but he seemed as if he wouldn't harm me. Obviously, he cared for Elijah, and he'd yet to touch me or make any comment towards wanting me in any way.

I listened intently as the two talked, while I tried to stay invisible. I knew Elijah was happy with where I chose to wait. I wasn't sure what to feel about me knowing him from before, but that could easily explain why I felt so comfortable with him.

I tensed up when Kaleb asked if he could ask me a few questions. I nodded anyway, hoping Elijah would either stop any questions, or answer for me.

"Since Elijah isn't going to ask, I feel like we can't wait any longer to question you, Dawn. You hold some very important details that are vital for our investigation. Under normal conditions, I'd have you come into our office, but we can't. So instead, I'm going to use this little recorder here," Kaleb spoke, shaking a small silver device in front of him in my line of sight. "Elijah, you have to be quiet; no rude remarks."

"Yes, Sir," Elijah muttered, making Kaleb laugh and mutter something I was unable to catch.

"I'll try to make this as painless as possible," he began in a sympathetic tone. "I want the complete truth from you, Dawn. Let's start with your full name."

"Dawn Elizabeth Ellis," I answered, just loud enough for the device to be able to pick up.

"Current age?"

"Nineteen, I think. My birthday was in August. It's November now, from what I'm told."

"Who are your parents?"

"Joan and Quentin Ellis."

"When were you taken, and from where?" Kaleb shot off easily without pause.

"On my fourteenth birthday. He brought me dinner that night so I didn't have to cook, saying it was a birthday gift. I was hungry." I answered, trying to keep calm and collected so the memories wouldn't take over.

"Who is *he*?" Kaleb asked, leaning forward. "Who is the man who took you from your home while your mom was at work?"

"Morgan," I stated, trying my hardest to not let my hatred for the man come through. Elijah squeezed my hand as he remained quiet. "He tried to drag me out, but I fought until he drugged me."

"Where did Morgan take you?" Kaleb asked, sensing I wasn't going to continue on my own.

"I don't know. I woke up with my hands tied behind my back in a jail cell. There were no windows...no sounds," I answered, near tears. I leaned more into Elijah. I couldn't stop the words. I explained how Morgan and Galvin began my training almost immediately, even before the drugs were out of my system. How I was trained to do whatever was commanded of me with hardly any words said. I hated that feeling—of being used and abused. I could still feel their hands on my body as I unwillingly let them mold me to what they wanted.

I detailed how I was forced to do things no fourteen-year-old should even know about. I went on with how I was punished by being kicked, hit, and abused in every way possible. I had refused to cooperate with my captors, not giving into them at first. But week by week, the weaker I got from the lack of food, I couldn't hold on to the fighting.

"Why was I taken?" I asked. "Do you know? Why me?"

"I'm assuming you were seen as an easy target," Elijah answered. "Many young girls are drawn away from their family by an unfilled promise of a man. What Morgan did was wrong. You know that, right?"

"I guess so," I knew it wasn't right, but no one had come and saved me. No one had been able to find me.

"People were looking for you," Elijah said, as though he could read my mind. "I tried to help find you. I went on every fucking search group there was to track you down. You are the reason I joined the FBI. I wanted to bring justice to the people who deserved it. Morgan is one of those people I'm going to bring down."

"So, you were forced to have sex?" Kaleb said, eyeing me sadly, and getting back on track.

"Yes." I was surprised the tears hadn't fallen from my eyes. I wanted to be done, to forget all about what I had been through.

"Good girl," Elijah whispered in my ear. I could feel him stiffen under me as he fought and lost the battle against speaking.

"Thank you," Kaleb said, shutting off the recorder. "You did a great job with answering me. I'll give you two a few minutes to relax while I make sandwiches for us to eat." He then got up and left us there in the comforting silence of Elijah's office.

"You did wonderfully," Elijah said, hugging me closely. "I'm so proud of you. I want to fuck up those men for hurting you," he added hoarsely.

My tears finally fell. I tried to get as close to him as I possibly could. I felt better having my story out there; I knew Morgan was going to get what he deserved, and felt good that I would have a part in that.

"Do you think my mother knew?" I asked, afraid of the answer.

"I saw her a few times, and just recently. I truly don't think she had any idea what Morgan was capable of, but who knows. She has changed a lot from when I was younger," Elijah replied.

"Why does that man care? Why do *you* care?" I asked shyly. Did I really want to know the answer?

"I care about people in general, but having known you before everything happened to you, it just makes me care more about you than the other people I help. Since I care so much, that means Kaleb cares, too. We are best friends—practically family. That's what friends should do: care for one another."

He paused, letting me think on that. It made sense; I just wasn't used to being cared for.

"Now, how about we go see what Kaleb whipped up for us?" He patted my leg as an indication that I should stand.

"Okay, Sir," I said, as I slowly made my way off his lap.

He took my hand with a smile and led me to the kitchen. I didn't really want to leave this room; I wanted to stay on his lap in his arms forever. Instead, I shuffled behind him as he led me into the kitchen, where three places were set with a simple sandwich and a glass of water. Kaleb had just finished setting the water down before taking a seat on one side of the table.

"Perfect timing," he grinned. Elijah let me sit first before taking a seat next to me, and across from Kaleb.

"Thank you, Kaleb," Elijah said before digging into his food. I slowly began to eat, not entirely hungry.

"No problem," he replied between bites. "Did you happen to look out the window? You have a guest waiting in your driveway."

"Crap," Elijah said roughly. "I ignored a phone call earlier today. Excuse me. I'll be back shortly."

Once Elijah left, Kaleb seemed to be in deep thought as he took a drink. I ate half of my sandwich before laying it down and putting my hands in my lap. I felt awkward. I had just gotten used to being here, with just Elijah and myself, even though it had been such a short time.

I wasn't sure why, but something about Kaleb demanded my training to the front of my mind.

"You know, Dawn, not many would have had the strength to go through what you did. You have suffered so much, yet you are still so strong," Kaleb said. He moved to sit beside me, ignoring the fearful look sure to be on my face. "You did wonderfully. I know the girl Elijah adored as a child is still inside you. I know the real you is in there. Right now, I know you are scared and not sure who you are, but given time, you will figure it out."

Sometime during his talk, he had taken my hand in his, and tears began to run down my cheeks. His simple, light touch made me try to jerk away from him. He lightly squeezed my hand, seeming to understand my problem.

"I really want you to get to a point where you can put some sort of trust in me, or at least my wife, so you can feel comfortable in my home as well as Elijah's. My wife, Kelly, and you could get along very well if given the chance. I will bring her by in a week or two, but she's not quite up to visiting yet."

"How is she doing?" Elijah said, making me jump. I

wasn't expecting him to be back. "I'm sorry I wasn't able to stop by; I wanted to."

"This girl here is more important than we are, as far as you're concerned. She might singlehandedly be able to bring down this sex ring," Kaleb said as he placed his folded hands on the table. "Kelly's doing better, but she's still sore and tired. The birth was very hard on her, but considering how the entire pregnancy went, it's not surprising."

"Good to hear. Please tell her I asked about her," Elijah said, as he ran his fingers down the length of my hair. I closed my eyes at his touch, feeling the gentleness I craved more than I wanted to admit.

"You two work out perfectly," Kaleb smiled. "Even with such an age difference."

"Whatever, Mr. Matchmaker," Elijah laughed. "I'm taking it one day at a time. Anyway, Morgan left. I told him Dawn wasn't here and I'd meet up with him later. Not sure what he wanted."

"What did you do?" Kaleb asked, his voice filled with concern.

I glanced at Elijah, noticing his hand was red and already slightly swollen.

"Uh," he began to answer. "Punched Morgan. All in a day's work."

"Why?" I asked, not sure why he'd go to such lengths.

"I couldn't shoot him, although I wanted to do just that," Elijah answered with a shrug.

"I wouldn't have told anyone," Kaleb joked.

"You know I can't shoot him, even though I want that man dead."

"I'm hoping we can get this case closed within the next three months. But I'd better head home to check on my girls. This is the first time in two weeks she's been able to be by herself. My sister was staying with us, but she had to get back to her store in New York," Kaleb said as he stood. "Oh, before

I forget…here, sweet girl. You deserve this, and so much more. It's just a little present."

He handed me a small silver charm bracelet with an attached charm. Elijah said, "That's a symbol of strength on there. You can add more as you decide what else symbolizes you."

When I looked up from my bracelet, he was gone, and Elijah looked at me in a way I wasn't used to. It was a mix of love and hope.

CHAPTER 10

ELIJAH

I was glad Kaleb took charge of the questioning. On cases where I was involved, I was usually the one who asked questions and gathered all the important information. People just knew I wasn't someone to mess around with. But when it came to the ones I cared about and loved? Well, it could get complicated.

I wanted so badly to pound a skull or two. Dawn was able to answer and give us more than enough information to bring the trafficking ring down. I knew it wouldn't be long now. We had evidence from two witnesses, plus Zack and my own recounts of the inner workings.

Galvin was a small-time mafia boss. He thought he was such a high guy, but really, he had more enemies than he knew what to do with. That's how I gained most of his trust: making him think I could keep the feds, and the rats, off his back. Sure, he could easily end my life, but so could any stranger on the street, so I wasn't worried about what he would do to me if I failed him. Plus, I'm good at what I do.

Dawn did much better than a lot of people would have if they were in her place. I wasn't all too surprised by what she had gone through at the hands of so many men. I had been with this case long enough to know how things were handled. I just never expected to find the one person I thought I'd never see again.

I wasn't happy that Morgan—the one who stole my girl—was watching my house when he thought I wasn't at home. It wasn't the first time, nor would it be the last. Working with the FBI, one could never be too careful when you had to go undercover so often. I had an alarm set up so a person would need a password to get in. I did have a number of safe houses I could go to when I was doing my part, but this was my home. I'd never had an issue before with being tracked back here.

I know he was worried about what I could do since I had a number of connections, and could easily make his life a living hell. He ended up getting roped into the mafia by mistake, and it was too late to get out by the time he noticed.

It was too late for anyone in the mafia world if they were in the *family*.

So, of course, I couldn't help but ask about his involvement in a roundabout way when I went out and met him in my driveway.

"So, Dawn said that you helped in her training," I hinted, keeping my voice calm and collected even though my blood was boiling with rage. I stuffed my hands into my pockets to keep myself from smashing his face in.

"Oh, ah . . . yeah, I guess I did," Morgan had replied timidly. "Um, how did that come up?"

"I just asked who did the wonderful training. She really is an ideal sub for me." I answered easily, the lie rolling smoothly off my tongue. "Just a few things here and there that need to be tweaked, but it won't take too much time to get her where I want her."

"Oh, well, yeah. I trained a handful of the girls, and Galvin

loved to watch each and every one. He's never touched any of them for some reason, but told the girls what he expected out of each of them."

"Where did you find her, anyway? She said something about being there for quite some time," I said.

"Her mother had a debt to repay. Did you know her? Joan Ellis?"

I knew Joan had worked as a waiter at a strip club Morgan had helped to look after, and owned by a Galvin Brown. It didn't pay that great, but Joan refused the help my parents offered

"She hasn't said anything about her parents, but yes, I do know her. I thought her daughter was a runaway," I said, giving the false conclusion of the case.

"Yes. I made sure it would look as such. Joan, of course, had to make the call to make it seem like the child was gone, so the school wouldn't ask questions. Now she's moved in with me and quit her job at the club, she wants her daughter back. Of course, she had no idea I was involved in any way, so I had a guy say something about the girl being found, he's so desperate to get into the ring, he would do anything," he laughed. I could hear a lie underneath his voice.

He was too easy to get information out of. Plus, he thought I was his 'friend', since I'd covered him on a few things to gain his trust as well. I sometimes wondered how he made it into the mob with his dimwitted brain.

"She was asking for help to find her daughter, but I couldn't help her out there, since you know, I really don't know where her daughter could possibly be," I said, trying to lay the sarcasm on thickly.

"So, have you tried her out yet? She's an amazing lay, if I do say so myself," Morgan said, a glint in his eyes at just the thought.

Without a thought, I punched Morgan. My fist connected against his jaw. His head turned with the force, his body falling into the side of his car, leaving a dent in his wake.

"Don't talk about Dawn that way. Ever," I said, my voice as

77

deadly as it had ever been before. No one would ever dare talk about my girl like that again—not if they wanted to live.

My fist hurt, but I was sure Morgan would fare worse.

I helped her with the small bracelet shortly after Kaleb left. She didn't say a word, but I could see her mind going over what he'd told her. Knowing she was tired, both physically and mentally, I decided on watching a movie.

Pulling her into my side after grabbing the throw blanket and tossing it over her legs so she could get comfortable, I chose a movie that looked to be a good to me, and something Dawn might also enjoy. I didn't really pay attention to it as it played, more concerned about her. I wanted so badly to help her in some way, but I knew she needed to come to terms with things first.

Dawn made her way to my lap, laying her head atop my thighs, and I couldn't stop the urge to play with her hair. Most women loved it, and I always enjoyed doing it.

I knew, in time, the real Dawn would come out. With love and support, she would overcome the darkest part of her life.

CHAPTER 11

DAWN

As the weeks went on, Elijah went back to work. He made sure to wake me before he left, letting me know who was downstairs. Most of the time, it was Joslyn. I liked her. She never pushed me to talk, but talked to me as often as she could. She'd talk about volunteering at the women's shelter and about her hobbies. I was finally starting to feel like I belonged here as a person, instead of a slave.

Emily had only been there a few times. She helped me get the laundry done, saying it kept her mind busy. She never talked about her past, but more of the future, and what she hoped to be able to do someday. She was currently taking online classes to get a website design program going. She'd ask me things here and there, but never really tried to keep a conversation up once I answered her questions. She was a private type of person, which I could understand. I didn't want to talk about my past, either.

I'm sure I wasn't much help. The list Elijah had given me to do was easy and didn't take much energy to complete. I was lost in my thoughts, trying to make sure everything was as expected. I didn't know how to make the two women who kept watch over me understand that I wasn't the type to talk. I liked to stay unseen.

Joslyn had brought over some books, but none of them held my attention. Sure, they were better than those Elijah had, but I wasn't a fan of romance or thriller novels. I did enjoy the puzzles she brought. Elijah even ordered a puzzle table for me to use that fit nicely underneath the couch when I wasn't working on one.

I didn't get to see much of Elijah, since he seemed to work late or was in his office most of the time, and I didn't want to disturb him. I'd keep the TV on whatever channel was last left on, not really watching it, but more for a background noise. I did wonder if I had done something wrong because Elijah seemed to be so distant after returning to work. I couldn't help but think maybe he just wasn't attracted to me.

The nights he would come to bed, he'd pull me to his chest and hold me safely all night long, as I'd taken to sleeping in his bed. But the nights he didn't come, I hardly got any sleep, as I was worried about what he was doing.

One windy night, the trees blew leaves against the side of the house. I had given up on sleep. I was planning on going to Elijah in his study and just kneel by him, letting him know I was able to please him in any way he'd like.

I was shocked when I heard voices in the office from the bottom of the staircase. The only lights that were on were in the study, so I stayed in the shadows so I could see who was there.

Keeping my back against the wall, I quietly made my way towards the office. I could see Elijah leaning against his desk. He wore the same jeans and a gray shirt he'd had on when he came home. Since the chairs were facing him, I couldn't see who it was he was talking to. His face wasn't happy—he was scowling, and he looked tired and stressed.

"So why did you have to come here?" Elijah sounded agitated. "I have more than enough to deal with."

"I didn't know who else I could talk to. That woman is getting some sort of idea in her head that you can get her daughter to her without being found out," I heard Morgan say. His voice sent shivers of fear through my body.

"I could, but I won't risk my job to do that. Plus, I'd be out money. I don't spend my money on things I don't intend to keep," Elijah seethed. His voice held a dark promise I knew never to test. "That woman knew what would happen long before it did."

"But she's changed. She quit her job and turned her life around. Doesn't Joan deserve a chance to see her daughter again? I can pay you for your trouble, Eli," Morgan almost begged.

I covered my mouth, trying to stop any noise that may escape.

"I ain't gonna sell my girl," Elijah laughed, letting his heavy accent slip through. "You know, you're being watched, so I really would advise you to not have her there anyway."

"I'm not worried about being found out," Morgan replied easily. "But at least let me see the girl so I can take a pic of her to show her mother."

"Absolutely not," Elijah huffed, standing up straight.

"Fine," Morgan grumbled, rubbing his jaw where the fading bruise no doubt lay. "But don't be surprised if Joan shows up wanting more help. She knows you can get her something."

"But I won't," Elijah said. "Now, I think it's best you leave."

"If I don't?"

"Then you can meet my fist again," Elijah said without a beat.

Having heard enough, I made my way back up the stairs,

just as quietly as I came down. I reached the landing at the same moment Elijah and Morgan entered the foyer.

It wasn't long before Elijah came up and took a shower before making his way to bed. I wasn't sure if he knew I was awake or not. I stayed still as he slid in behind me, wrapping an arm around my waist and burying his nose in my hair. It didn't take him long to fall asleep. His breathing evened out, and I closed my own eyes, hoping his presence would calm me enough to allow some sleep for myself.

∼

The room was dim as I was shoved from behind. I wore the thin dirty white gown I was forced to put on when I was brought to this place. I wasn't sure how long I had been here, as there were no windows or clocks. I had to squint to see into the room, and hope to not injure myself on anything. My body was already sore due to the hits and kicks for not wanting to obey the men's every command. I was sure my ribs were broken.

The room was small but held a small stained mattress in the far corner. The ugly yellow paint was peeling off the walls.

"All yours, buddy," Morgan laughed with another push on my back. He blocked the doorway so I couldn't try to run. None of these rooms had doors, so anyone who was walking by could watch the happenings in each room.

I finally looked up and saw the one man I had hoped to never see, let alone be in the same room with. His dark eyes were clouded by whatever drug he was on. His overly long dark blond hair was pulled back into a neat and clean low ponytail. He wore a low-riding pair of blue jeans that were stained and ripped in places, along with a black shirt with a lot of holes.

He smirked as he looked me up and down. "How old is this one?" he asked as he began to rub his crotch with his palm.

"Fourteen," Morgan replied. "She's feisty."

"A young one."

"Yeah. Galvin plans to keep this one. The money she'll bring in will be great," Morgan said. "I offered to do the deed, but he insisted you had to be the one."

"Now, girl, you behave and let me do as I wish," Erick said, not taking his eyes off me.

"You're not gonna touch me," I said, with as much anger as I possibly could, while I tried to find a way out of this small room, my heart pounding in fear.

Erick just laughed as he slowly stalked me around the room. I ended up falling backward onto the bed as he caged me in with his body.

"That wasn't hard, now," he said as he advanced towards me. He towered over me. I scooted back to the wall as much as I could.

He easily grabbed my ankles in a tight grip and jerked me down the bed. I screamed in fear. His knees pushed my own apart as far as they would go. I tried to hit and kick him, push him away, but it only made his eyes darken before he pinned my hands above my head.

"Just relax and don't fight me. It won't hurt . . . much," he smiled as he undid his pants.

∼

I SAT UP IN BED, GASPING. IT WAS LIGHT OUT AND THERE WAS NO Elijah in bed beside me; his side was cold. I was sweaty, my hair sticking to my neck. I hoped a shower would calm my panic.

I took my time, knowing that whoever was on company duty wouldn't mind me taking a little extra time. I almost wished, in a way, that no one was there. I wanted to be alone, but at the same time not.

The shower helped some, even though the remains of the nightmare were still on the edge of my thoughts. The nightmares seemed to be coming more often than I liked. I could still feel Erick's hands on my body, no matter how hard I scrubbed my skin.

I made my way downstairs to where the smell of bacon and eggs was coming from. I left my hair down, as I wasn't good at doing anything with it like Elijah could. I was tempted to ask if I could cut it, but wasn't sure if he would approve.

I was disappointed he didn't wake me up that morning. The house was quiet, but I figured Joslyn would be waiting in the kitchen for me. I was surprised when, instead of Joslyn sitting at the table, Elijah was. He was reading the newspaper and still in his pj.'s. A plate of bacon and eggs sat at the spot beside him.

"Good morning, kitten," he smiled over the paper. "Come eat."

I slowly made my way to the chair beside him, confused as to why he was home. I slowly ate the food, noticing it had just been made shortly before I came down the stairs, as it was still warm.

"How did you sleep?" he asked, laying the paper down.

"Fine, Sir," I lied. It was better sleep than I got in the cell, so I couldn't complain—even with the nightmares.

"Hmm. You slept later than you have all week," he replied, looking at me with those brown eyes. "Do you feel unwell? You're a little pale."

"Had a bad dream," I whispered with a shrug. "But I'm fine."

"I'm here if you want to talk," Elijah said, taking his empty plate away. "I'm sorry I haven't been home much. I've been trying to get this case closed as soon as possible, and because of that, I've slacked on my duties to take care of you. Emily said you haven't been doing well because of me not being here?"

"I've been fine," I said. I usually always got lost in my mind; plus, Emily hadn't been here much.

"If you say so," he said, giving me a look that said he didn't believe me. "Anyway, Kaleb and his wife will be by in a little bit."

Not knowing what to say, I chose to stay quiet. I was worried Elijah may have heard me last night. And if he did, would I be punished? Would Kaleb's wife be nice, or expect anything from me?

"Something's bothering you," Elijah said, kneeling so he was eye level with me, while I sat still in my chair. His eyes were probing my own.

I vaguely remembered a boy with the same colored eyes, and the same look, telling me hundreds of times that my eyes were the window to my soul. The boy was older but seemed to help me get what I was feeling out in the open with just that one look. This time, although it was no different, I changed the subject.

"We did know each other; I remember small things," I said, tilting my head to the side. I knew him, but how well was that?

"Of course, we did," Elijah replied as his look softened. "You used to follow me everywhere, and would pretty much do anything I wanted you to do…except for going away." He smiled.

"I can remember your eyes," I said, looking up at him through my eyelashes.

"You would get upset a lot when Zack and I didn't want to play with you. I was fourteen at the time. Zack didn't like the idea of you being seen by our friends when we played with you. I always convinced you to wait until later. You had me wrapped around your finger; you still do," Elijah said tenderly. "I'll have Joslyn bring some pictures over, and she can tell the stories that go with each one.

"Now, I'm going to go get dressed. You may go do whatever it is that you do after you eat breakfast."

"Yes, Sir," I said, glad I had been able to get out of

answering Elijah for the time being. I was sure he'd bring it up again at some point.

"You don't have to keep calling me 'Sir'," Elijah demanded.

"Sorry," I mumbled with a small blush.

He gave me a smile before heading upstairs. I tidied up the kitchen before making my way to the living room, checking everything was clean and put away.

CHAPTER 12

ELIJAH

Joan was asking too many questions for my liking. She had stopped at the FBI office more times than I could count, asking anyone and everyone where to get an address or phone number for her daughter. She had tried to corner me a time or two, but I didn't budge. She even went as low as to flirt with me to get information.

All it did was make me shudder.

Joan knew that I had assumptions that she was behind Dawn's disappearance. Of course, she didn't seem too concerned that I knew. Guess all the years of drug use was starting to show by her confused way of thinking.

I had this gut feeling she was up to something that would cause us all trouble.

At least half the time when she showed up, I could tell she was high on something. It seemed to make her more adamant about finding Dawn. Mike was getting sloppy and panicky every time he'd see me, so I knew he was up to something. It was only a matter of time before he'd slip.

I was tired. *Beyond* tired. I felt bad that I hadn't really spent much time with Dawn, but I also did tell her when I brought her to my house that I worked a lot of hours. I had to keep looking over the evidence that had been gathered.

Because of Mike and Joan, Kaleb was making me take paid time off, saying I was removed from the case until it was closed. I was still on the case under the table. I was in too deep with my undercover rule to just step out. I couldn't pull out of the mafia without paying with my life.

I wasn't pleased with Morgan when he showed up late last night. He was lucky I was still up, finishing rewriting a report for an interview on another case. I was tired and wanted to lie next to her, wrapping her safely in my arms.

Morgan looked tired and desperate. Joan was hounding him about wanting him to do something about her daughter. There wasn't much I could do, but I told him I would see if I could at least a get a picture. There was something he wasn't telling me. He seemed too interested in wanting to see Dawn, even offering to pay for her. I wasn't going to let him anywhere near her if I could help it.

Kaleb had come up with the idea of a picture of the girl to send to her mother, to hopefully give her some sort of relief. I was worried about letting Dawn call her mother, as I wasn't sure how she felt about Joan. I also didn't want to risk Joan tracing the phone back to me, or upsetting Dawn. I knew when Dawn had come down the stairs. I could feel her there in the shadows. I didn't think she'd heard too much, and wanted to keep the truth of her mother from her. Joan was nothing like I remembered, but that could easily be explained by the disappearance of her daughter—and the drugs that she was addicted to.

The next morning, I woke up with her leg thrown over my own, and I had to wield my erection away. With a deep breath, I slowly made my way out from under her and left her to sleep.

I was more than okay with Kaleb and his wife coming over when he'd called earlier that morning, figuring it should have been sooner than now, but today worked perfectly.

When I came down from getting dressed, I saw her sitting on the couch with her head down. *Was this what she did every day?* The house was all cleaned, so I knew she'd done everything and more than I'd lined out for her to do.

"So, what do you do all day while I'm gone?" I asked as I took a seat next to her on the loveseat.

"Clean, mostly," she replied.

"You must do more than that?" I asked, looking her up and down. Her shoulders were hunched in.

"Puzzles. Read a little. I don't really care for the books Joslyn brought over," she answered, wrinkling her nose. I thought it was adorable, and couldn't help but smile.

"Well, what kind of books do you like?" I asked, taking a seat next to her.

"Nothing that's here," she pouted, but kept her eyes down.

I gave out a laugh, making her quickly look at me in shock. "Sorry, but that's the most emotion I've gotten from you all week. I ordered you some books you may like better. They should be here in a few days."

She just glared at me, but soon returned her gaze back to her lap. I had ordered some of the top sellers in a few different sections.

"Joslyn did say you were good at puzzles," I said, trying to get more out of her. "Why aren't you doing one now?

"You have company coming over," she replied. "You said you wanted the living room clean when you went over the rules."

"A puzzle or a few books out would be okay," I sighed. "What did you do when you were alone before you came here?"

"Nothing. Maybe sleep if I could. Sometimes dream about

what would happen if I wasn't there," she answered. "I even made up stories in my head to pass the time."

"I'm sorry for what you've been through," I said, kissing the side of her head. "If you want to write anything that you came up with, I will be more than happy to get you some paper and a pen."

The doorbell rang through the house, and I went to answer it with Dawn quietly following me. Opening the door, there stood Kaleb and Kelly. Kelly had her shoulder length blond hair pulled pack in a half ponytail. They were both dressed in comfortable clothes. He held a diaper bag and a car seat that was covered with a soft green blanket.

I welcomed them in, hearing Dawn scamper towards the kitchen and out of sight. After giving Kelly a quick hug, I pointed them to the living room, before finding out where Dawn was hiding.

"Dawn?" I called as I entered the kitchen. I found her leaning against the counter with her head in her hands. Her shoulders were shaking, but she wasn't making any sound. "Hey, what's going on?" I gently laid my hands on her thin shoulders.

"I'm sorry, Sir," she gasped as she took in short, shaky breaths.

I pulled her to me, wrapping my arms around her shaking form, trying to give her comfort. I tried to wrack my brain as to why she was upset, but came up empty.

It took Dawn a few minutes to calm down. Slowly, she regained even breathing. I allowed her a few more minutes so she could hopefully sort out her thoughts. Once she appeared calmer, I lifted her face with both of my hands cupping her jawline so I could meet her eyes.

"Do you mind telling me what's going on in that head of yours?" I asked, staring into her panicked brown eyes.

"I'm sorry," she breathed out, closing her eyes.

"Answer me, please, Dawn," I coaxed. Her green eyes

were outlined in red from her crying and panic. I was trying extremely hard to not sound demanding when I asked her to do something. She could easily just tell me go to hell, and I'd be happy.

"When . . . he invited people, it was never a good thing for me. And . . . I just thought I'd have to do . . ."

"You will never be with anyone in this house like that," I said sternly. "If, and that's a big 'if', we are ever in a relationship later on down the road, I don't share. You have no reason to worry about issues like that here, all right?"

"I'm sorry," she replied, leaning her forehead against my chest.

"No worries," I said. "You can always come to me with any concerns or questions. There will not be any sort of punishment. Now, how about we go see our guests?"

"Okay, Sir," she said, taking a deep breath. When she met my eyes, I could see she was calmer, but also locked down with her emotions. Deciding to let that slide for now, even though I enjoyed being able to see how she felt at certain times, I wrapped my arm loosely around her waist and led her to the living room.

Kaleb and Kelly were sitting on the couch and smiled when we entered.

"Dawn, you remember Kaleb," I introduced. "And this is Kelly, his wife."

"Hey, Sug," she greeted in a soft voice that was heavily accented. "And this little thing is Lilly." She indicated to the baby lying in her lap, wrapped in a light pink blanket.

I sat down on the loveseat, where Dawn perched as close to me as she possibly could.

"Lilly is four weeks old now," Kaleb said proudly, with a wide grin.

"She's a fighter," Kelly said, still just as softly. "There were so many times I thought she wouldn't make it, but she did. And she's as healthy as can be."

"I'm glad everything worked out. How are you doing? Kaleb said the birth was hard on you," I said as Dawn wrapped an arm around my elbow.

"Yes—a very long labor. At first, I refused the idea of a C-section. The epidural slowed my progress and made my blood pressure unstable. I can't remember some things. Plus, having low iron on top of everything didn't help matters." Kelly answered. "But she came out with a tiny cry and all pink. I had to stay in the hospital for three nights, to get my iron levels up, along with getting the hang of moving around with stitches and staples. I'm still tired, but doing so much better every day."

"Glad to hear it," I answered. I knew from my mom's recounts that having a baby, and the first few weeks after, were the hardest. "I wanted to come see you, but I had important matters to attend to."

"No worries, Elijah," she replied. "Kaleb briefly explained the protection detail."

"Wanna hold Lilly?" Kaleb asked my girl, whose eyes were glued to the baby. She shook her head before pressing herself into my shoulder.

"I'd like to," I stated. My mother had brought small children over from the said shelter when there wasn't enough room. She'd sometimes bring kids of all ages into our home, where, no matter what the age they were, they seemed to look up at me like an idol.

Kaleb took the baby from Kelly and brought her to me. Her eyes slowly blinked opened as she was moved from her napping place. I held her with her head in my right arm. Lilly was small and adorable, and she looked like her mama.

"I'm surprised you don't have any kids yet," Kaleb joked.

"I hadn't found the perfect mother," I shrugged. I tended to be a child magnet, but I didn't mind. I saw Dawn peek at the bundle, even though she was trying to be sneaky about it.

"Do you want kids, Dawn?" Kaleb asked, making her jump.

"I don't know, Sir," she answered quietly, briefly looking at him.

"You have time to figure it out, Sug. No one expects you to answer right now, anyway," Kelly stated, shooting Kaleb a glare.

"I don't know if I can," she sighed, looking at the baby and touching her feet.

"What do you mean by that?" I asked gently. Now was probably not the best time, but Kelly would be able to help if needed. I wasn't the best with girl talk or girl problems, and this was obviously a girl thing.

"I was pregnant . . . once. It was shortly after the first time Erick had me. When they noticed, they . . . they hit me in my stomach until I bled down there. Erick and the others were careful after that to make sure I didn't get pregnant again." She didn't take her eyes off the baby.

"Oh, Dawn," Kelly said, coming over to the couch beside her. Dawn jumped slightly, not expecting it. "I lost a few myself, and I did everything the doctors told me to do. It took years to finally be able to have this one, and it will mostly likely be my only child. Which is more than fine with me. I may not have been through what you have, but I can sympathize with you. I will always listen if you want to talk," she went on, wrapping her arm around my girl.

"Thanks, I think," Dawn mumbled. "Maybe sometime."

"Anytime, Sug."

"Here, you can hold her," I said, handing the little one to Dawn once I got my arm free from her. I gently showed her on how to hold her, supporting her head just right in her elbow. Dawn was wide eyed with shock and nerves. Meeting her eyes, I smiled, letting her know she was doing fine. Dawn slowly looked down at the baby, who was staring up at her.

"I was terrified the first time I held her. I had to pick her up to give her over to Kelly once we were put into our own room at the hospital," Kaleb said as he leaned forward. "The nurses had given us privacy for a few hours for her to rest after her surgery."

"He couldn't figure out how to change her diaper at first, either," Kelly laughed.

"Diapers," Kaleb grumbled, shaking his head and glaring at the idea, which made me laugh. In turn, the baby began to cry. I was happy to see my girl didn't panic, but she did look to Kelly to find out what to do.

"She's hungry," Kelly said as she reached for the diaper bag on the coffee table. She made up a bottle and then explained to Dawn how to feed the wailing girl.

"You're a natural," I said, leaning to whisper in her ear. "I'll do whatever it takes, see any doctor, to find out if you can have a baby if you ever want to."

"So, are you enjoying your time off work?" Kaleb asked after a few quiet minutes.

"The last three weeks were productive and busy, but I'm glad to be home now," I answered.

"Good. I do have some news for you, but only for you. I don't think the ladies of the house need to hear," Kaleb said, hinting towards the office. I kissed Dawn on the side of her head before I made my way, following Kaleb and closing the door behind me.

CHAPTER 13

DAWN

I was in awe, and couldn't believe I was allowed to hold the baby. She was so little. I had no idea what I was doing, and was more than glad they showed me what to do. Holding Lilly, all my panic disappeared; having something to focus on helped. I couldn't resist giving a little smile as Kaleb joked about not knowing what to do at first, either.

Elijah's whispered words shocked me, and I wasn't sure what to do about it. I wasn't sure if I could have kids, let alone even want any. Could I see myself ever having any of my own? I wasn't sure. I didn't know if I wanted to have a baby to begin with.

"Who do you think you can trick?" Erick snarled as he stormed into the cell where I was huddled into the corner by the sink. I had taken to hiding there after Morgan had dragged me back *after I was used by some nameless man. I was fifteen, and my stomach was beginning to swell.*

"Erick," Morgan warned.

"Don't even start. You know she can't be pregnant," Erick yelled. "I don't know how Galvin had let this go on for so long."

"She wasn't showing until this week, Erick," Morgan said calmly. "You don't need to do it this way."

"No spawn of mine is allowed to leave this place," Erick sneered as he lifted me up from the floor by my hair. He punched my slightly rounded stomach, knocking the breath out of me. I fell to the floor, gasping tearfully, where he then kicked me over and over until Morgan pulled him away and shoved him out the door. I couldn't move as I sobbed in pain.

"I'm sorry, child," Morgan said as he injected something into my arm after kneeling next to me. "I would have made sure it would have gone to a good home."

Why was he so nice all of a sudden? He'd never given me such care, so what was he after? It wasn't just to save me, that's for sure.

At the time, I didn't know what was going on. I didn't understand that I was pregnant, or why I was being punished. I barely even knew what I was being forced to do. I just did what the men wanted so I wouldn't get hit or tied up all the time. Between the lack of sleep and food, everything seemed so dulled.

My hope was completely shattered when I woke some time later. I was covered in blood and after birth, and parts of the gown stuck to my skin. I shouldn't have taken a closer look.

There, laying surrounded by blood, was a lifeless little body. The fetus was twenty-nine weeks old. There was just skin and bones, and tiny like a baby doll would have been. It's toes and fingers still had webs as didgets.

I screamed and moved as far away as I could, but couldn't take my eyes off the thing. My screaming alerted Morgan, who had been out in the hall.

He was in front of me, silencing me by kissing me. He always liked to kiss me, saying he would be my Daddy, and save me from this hell when I was no longer any use to Galvin. I wanted to spit in his face, but I had learned not to.

I hated it when he wanted me to call him Daddy.

"Hey now," he cooed after backing away and running his finger along my nose. His dark eyes glinted with something I couldn't name. Something that promised pain upon pain as he pretended to care. "None of that. We don't want Erick knowing you're awake."

"You don't have to answer, but how old were you when you lost your baby?" Kelly asked quietly, bringing me out of my thoughts.

"Fifteen," I answered after a pause. "It never happened again. Morgan made sure."

"What do you mean by that?" she asked, her voice soft.

"He'd give me injections of something," I answered. I hated those shots. They made me sick for a day afterward.

"The depo shot," she said but continued, seeing I was confused. "It's a shot that prevents pregnancies and stops the monthly menstrual cycle."

"Oh," I said, wrinkling my nose. That could make sense; my periods were very light, if I even had one.

"So, how do you like it here? I know where you were before, but not all your history," she said. I watched in fascination as she easily removed the wet diaper and put a new one on Lilly.

"It's warmer here," I answered, bringing my legs up to my chest. "And I can have food."

"What's your favorite food?"

"Everything . . . but cheese sandwiches. That's the only thing I got to eat there. Dried, moldy bread, and cheese," I replied, feeling at ease with her.

"Understandable," she said. "Have you been outside at all?"

I shook my head. It really didn't occur to me to even ask or to try. I missed the sun and the fresh air, but I could live with just staying in the window to get whatever I could.

"We'll have to change that once we have better weather. It's pretty chilly out this time of year," Kelly said. "But you do need a swimsuit so you can use Elijah's pool."

"What?" I asked, shocked. "I . . . I can't swim."

"Oh, Sug," Kelly said softly, laying a hand over my own. "It doesn't matter if you can swim or not; the pool is only five feet deep, so no worries. There's also a hot tub that fits at least ten people."

"Oh . . ." I replied with wide eyes. I'd never been in a pool or a hot tub. The idea sounded appealing—if Elijah allowed me to.

"I'll be right back. I'm going to go grab Eli's laptop so we can order you some clothes. I expect you need things men don't really think about," Kelly smiled and stood. "If Lilly cries, you can pick her up, okay?"

I simply nodded, still stuck on the idea of being able to do something I wanted to do. I didn't expect Kaleb and Kelly to be so nice. They made me feel included, like I belonged. Morgan was the only one who had been halfway nice to me, even though he was also the one who made me do things I didn't want to, and the one that took me from my home. He seemed like he couldn't decide how to handle me. When we were alone, Morgan was nice, and almost sweet and tender. He would teach me how to please Master Galvin the best, and how to stay on his good side.

Then when he was there, among others, he'd ignored me or egg people on, alongside Galvin. On many accounts, Morgan was the one being egged on and he never once seemed to care what he was doing to me, even when I was crying and begging him to stop. He'd use me, hit me, and yell at me, making me dig myself more and more into the pit of darkness. He used me for sex, just like the others.

Kelly was back shortly, holding Elijah's computer. She checked on her baby before sitting back down next me. She opened the lid and entered into some store's website, as she explained the whole thing to me on how to get there. We spent some time looking at the different clothes and styles. Kelly let me pick what I wanted and liked, not once saying anything about what I couldn't have. I found a cute two-piece tank top type swimsuit with shorts in a dark purple color. It was simple and covered much more than most of the styles that she pointed out to me. I also picked out some shorts, tank tops, pj's, pants, sweaters, and shirts that would last the winter.

"Once summer rolls around, we can order more summer clothes for you," Kelly said once she'd placed the order.

Elijah and Kaleb came back out of the office to join us, and said they were ordering pizza for a late lunch.

"So, how much am I out?" Elijah said through a laugh as he took his bank card from Kelly. He took a seat next to me again, pulling me to his side where I didn't complain. He made me feel safe and protected.

"Three hundred," Kelly answered. "Not as much as I would spend in one order."

"That's it?" Elijah asked half shocked. "I figured with you, it would have been more."

"I could have easily, but it was tough enough to get Dawn to let me know what she liked. And most of its clothes and shoes she will need until summer. If she fills out any with the healthy diet, she may need a bigger size in a few months."

"Oh, by the way, Dawn, my dad sent a text to me, and all the results came back clean," Elijah said near my ear where only I could be able to hear him. "No STDs. You are borderline anemic, but that should get straightened out since you have a better diet. If not, you'll have to start taking iron pills."

I was glad there were no health issues I needed to worry about.

As they talked back and forth, I sat there quietly. I knew these three had a great friendship, and I envied that as I watched them joke with one another. With the envy, I felt guilt. I shouldn't be feeling jealous. I was a nobody. I didn't deserve to feel accepted; I was just a slave.

"Dawn?" Elijah said beside me.

I looked up at him, hoping to tamper down my feelings.

"Are you okay?" he asked, gently cupping my cheek in his palm. I leaned into it, closing my eyes at his touch. "What were you thinking about?"

The ringing of the doorbell saving me from having to come clean.

I excused myself to the bathroom.

I splashed my face with lukewarm water, hoping I could get my thoughts and emotions under control. I looked in the mirror; I couldn't see anything special about myself. My dull green eyes were lined with tiredness. My face was thin from lack of food but was just now starting to fill out, so it wasn't all just skin and bones. My black hair was half limp, half curly. It did have more shine than a few weeks ago. Sighing, I left the bathroom and followed the smell of pizza and the clatter the three made in the kitchen.

"Hey, Princess," Kaleb smiled as he noticed me at the kitchen entryway. "We got a plain pepperoni pizza, or a pizza that has all the works. Which do you want?"

"Pepperoni?" I answered—more of a question. I couldn't remember the last time I'd had pizza.

"Coming right up!" Kaleb smiled as he placed a piece of pizza and handed me a plate. I took a seat next to Elijah at the table, who was busy eating his own pizza, covered in many different types of meat and veggies.

I couldn't contain a small moan at my first bite. It was filled with cheese and flavor. Feeling eyes on me, I blushed as I looked up. Elijah was staring at me with surprise before he got his look under control.

"Um, good pizza?" He grinned while Kaleb laughed. At least Kelly would keep her thoughts on the matter to herself, although she was smiling while looking between the two of us.

"Yes, Sir," I said, looking back down at the pizza. I could feel my cheeks heat.

I made sure to not let any more sounds come out as I finished most of the piece.

"You done?" Elijah asked as Kelly got up to tend to her crying baby.

"Yes, Sir," I said. He instantly got up and took care of my plate before I had the chance. Once he'd put the dishes away, he led me back to the living room, where Kaleb and Kelly were sitting on the loveseat. I sat down next to Elijah, who didn't waste any time to wrap an arm around me. I leaned into him, feeling full and content.

"I can't believe we've been friends for almost seven years already," Kaleb said.

"If it weren't for you, Kaleb, I wouldn't be sitting here. I probably would have been stuck at an easy cop job," Elijah replied. "But I wouldn't change it for anything."

"Me either. I still can't get over the fact that you two knew each other from the BDSM club," Kelly said. "And I still want to see you two together sometime," she left off.

"Not gonna happen, sis," Elijah laughed good naturally. "I think I'm good where I am."

"You . . . what?" I asked, confused and shocked, looking between the two.

"He helped me learn to have control in a healthier way. He's a Dom, like myself, and once Kaleb met Kelly, he guided me into how to be one," Elijah asked. "Does that bother you?"

"No," I answered quickly.

"We don't share, with anyone, so it's just a fantasy that won't ever be fulfilled. I'm more than okay with that, since Kaleb is great at what he does. We do some scenes at the club sometimes, but haven't for over a year now," Kelly smiled up at Kaleb.

Of course, my face grew warm, and I hid it against Elijah's arm, making him laugh.

It wasn't long afterward the two guests left with their baby, leaving me half asleep as I laid my head in Elijah's lap. He played with my hair as he turned the TV on to the news. The sun had set a while ago, and I didn't want to move from this spot, enjoying the quiet of the house.

Here, I felt content, and almost safe. It wasn't something I would ever take for granted.

CHAPTER 14

DAWN

*E*lijah was home most of the time the following week, making it more enjoyable. He left once to go to the grocery store, after having me help come up with a list of items we needed. It truly didn't matter to me what he bought, as I would eat or try to cook just about anything. I normally cooked easy things that had the directions on the packages, since I had to teach myself how to cook. I had refused Joslyn's help, not wanting to take up more of her time than she was already giving up to stay with me. She'd brought a couple of cookbooks that were fairly easy for me to follow.

On the day he went out, Joslyn came over, along with Emily and Zack. I could tell something was up, as Emily was nervous and fidgety. Zack acted like there wasn't anything to worry about, sitting in the living room and playing on his phone.

Joslyn had brought a big dark green scrapbook full of pictures and was telling Emily and I some of the stories that went along with them. One set of pictures was of Elijah

103

holding a newborn baby who was sleeping and wrapped in pink. She had a small bow on her head. Zack sat beside Elijah, pouting and looking off to a different direction. They both had the same color of dark hair.

"Elijah was thrilled to finally hold you, Dawn. You were a week old, and he promised to protect you from the world that day," Joslyn had said, as she pointed to the picture. "Zack wanted nothing to do with you, and refused to let me take one good picture."

Emily gave out a laugh. "Just like now, you know if he's not happy if there's something wrong."

Another picture showed Elijah pushing me on a tire swing. The ground was covered in white flowers. My eyes were bright with happiness. Elijah, at the age of twelve, was happily pushing me, as I sat on the black tire swing tied with a heavy rope to the tree branch high above.

"You were about three here, and loved that tire swing. You would only let Elijah push you when we were all up at the cabin. Elijah said the swing was only for his girl," Joslyn said with a smile.

Another picture was of Elijah and Zack, with me sitting on a chair between them. Both boys had on matching Batman shirts, their hands in the pockets of their jeans. They didn't look too thrilled about the picture. I was a tired looking ten-year-old—a thing that became normal for me.

"You were upset because your father had died the night before, and your entire world was shifted. You wanted nothing to do with your mother, even though she was just out busy getting things in order for the funeral a few days later. Elijah stuck to your side, and helped you along so you weren't so sad," Joslyn said. "That was a tough time for all of us."

"Do you have any pictures of my parents?" I asked.

Zack looked up at me, shocked I'd asked. I guess I hadn't really talked much that day, and some days were quieter ones. And Elijah wasn't there. He smiled happily at me before turning back to his phone.

"Yes, of course," Joslyn answered as she began to shuffle some pages. "Ah, here is one of the last ones I was able to get."

My parents stood side by side, but not touching. My dad wore a long flannel shirt and a pair of stained pants. He had his fishing hat on, covering his black hair. His brown eyes were filled with laughter, but I could see a sadness behind it. His hair was cut short. My mother looked tired, but full of life. Her green eyes hid secrets, but determination. Her blonde hair was pulled back into a messy side bun. I looked nothing like her. I was pleased with that, but not entirely sure why.

"What was my dad like?" I asked, tracing his picture.

"He was full of life. He loved fishing and camping. He worked hard, but always made time for you," Joslyn answered, remembering better days. "I'll have to get some of the things he left you out of storage. He wanted to make sure you got some things your mother would have sold, since they do hold some value."

"She was a great mother to you," Elijah said as he entered the room and sat on the coffee table. "She made sure you came first. But when money got tighter, she got into some things that caused her priorities to change. She got into the wrong group of people; she had to pay off debts, and got in too deep. Quentin knew, and wasn't too pleased. Not only did she lose her priorities, but she also lost track of who she was. Drugs can cause all sorts of issues, no matter the person."

"Oh," I said, at a loss for words. I knew my dad was dead, but I couldn't quite get my mind to wrap around the idea that she could ever do anything like that. "Is that why she was with Morgan?"

"I'm not sure, but it's a good possibility," Elijah

answered, laying his hand over the one on my lap. "And for that reason, I haven't allowed your mother to know where you are. She knows you were found, but not by whom, and it must stay that way. You aren't a slave to be bought and sold to whoever has the most money. Joan has changed from when I knew her years ago, so I personally don't trust her, but if you want to call her, or even text her, I will be happy to get you a phone so you can. She's still with Morgan," he finished. His eyes were filled with worry and love as he looked at me.

"I don't know if I want to talk to her," I said, with tears in my voice. I blamed her a great deal for my kidnapping, as she was spending so much time with the one that took me, and was still with him.

"That's perfectly fine," Emily said, pulling me into a hug. "You have all the time you need."

"Well, until the trial comes up. You will have to talk and let the judge hear your side of things, and then, depending on how things go, you may want to go back to her," Zack stated sadly.

"No!" I said, eyes wide with panic. "I . . . I can't go back to her."

"Why not?" Elijah asked calmly as he moved to sit beside me.

"I . . . I think she had something to do with the planning for Morgan to take me. The week before my birthday, I overheard them talking about prices and methods of repayments. Could they have been talking about me?" I said in a near whisper.

"It's very likely. It's something we're looking into," Zack replied with a grimace.

"You are of age, so the state can't force you to go if you don't want to. You're welcome to stay here with me for as long as you'd like," Elijah said with determination.

"You could just get married," Zack laughed.

BROKEN REVIVAL

"No way," Elijah seethed. "I won't force you, Dawn, into anything like that."

"I know Elijah," I replied with a small smile. Although, I would, if it saved me from having to go with her. It was a gut feeling: I couldn't go with my mom, no matter what happened.

"Did you get your shopping done?" Joslyn asked as she closed the scrapbook and set it on the side table.

"For the most part," Elijah answered.

"Maybe Dawn will have to go with you when it's safe," Emily hinted.

"Hopefully that will be soon, so I can take her out and show her around," Elijah smiled. "We really aren't sure when that will be, since once the case is closed, it will go to trial, and then the news media will be all over her, wanting more details."

"We'll have that covered so no one bothers you at all," Zack grinned. "Emily will have to testify at the trial. So will you, Dawn, so you'll be safest with us wherever we go."

"Okay," I said, taking everything in. I was comfortable here. I didn't want to see those men, but knew I'd have to face them sometime—either here or somewhere else.

When I was first taken from Joan, I wanted her, begged to see her and go back to her. Now, after all this time, I wasn't sure I wanted anything to do with her. From what Elijah had said, she wasn't the same, and since I'd changed just by being here, things were different. I had a choice.

"Could my dad's murder be connected to Morgan, or even my mom?" I asked, hating the idea as I said it. I didn't think I could face my mother if she did have something to do with it, but it would explain why things happened the way they did.

"That's a good question—I hadn't thought of that," Elijah said, running a hand through his hair. "I'll give the idea to Kaleb when I talk to him next, and see what he can find. The killer was found not far that night from where it happened, but it's possible it's all connected. Your dad's body wasn't found, but presumed dead, with the amount of blood at the crime scene."

"Morgan may be able to tell you something if you ask," Zack said.

"Yeah, but I don't want to ask too many things. He may not be too bright, but since I've asked him a few things about Dawn already, I'm not sure how much will push him into suspecting something's up."

"Kaleb may come up with something better," Zack said as he helped Emily from the chair they were sitting on. "Come on, it's time to go."

I looked over at Emily and her nervousness was showing again—more so now. I reached over and squeezed her hand.

"I have a therapy session," Emily whispered.

"It was all her idea," Zack stated proudly with a smile. "She needs someone who can understand better than me, and to help her get over a few issues I have no idea how to handle."

"Yeah, but now I'm not so sure I can do this," she said, looking anywhere but at the people who were in the room.

"Of course you can," Joslyn said, just as proud. "You've been through so much, and you can do this."

CHAPTER 15

DAWN

*T*he next few days flew by. We got into a nice comfortable rhythm; I did the laundry and kept the house clean, and Elijah helped to an extent. Mostly, he just watched and talked to me. It didn't take long to make sure everything was in order. The items Elijah ordered, along with all the clothes Kelly had ordered for me, came in later that week. I was happy to have some new books I was actually interested in, and couldn't wait to read. They were mostly young adult ones, and a few life lesson books that helped me deal with some of my confusing thoughts and emotions.

I'd tried to help Elijah out a few times, sure he was in pain from his own hard issues, but he refused every time. I sure he wanted some sort of release from his morning wood. He made sure he was up and dressed before I was in the mornings, and by the time we went to bed, I was too tired to try too hard to give him some relief. I was scared to voice my thoughts but didn't know what else to do. I wanted to maybe talk to Emily or even Kelly, but neither had been by at a time we were left alone without Elijah in the same room for me to ask.

It wasn't until the following week that Kelly and Lilly came by to visit again. Elijah took that time to call Kaleb about a few new ideas on the case, as he hadn't had much of a chance since Kaleb had been busy and not in a place that he could talk about it over the phone.

I was glad I was getting more comfortable with handling the baby—even able to change a diaper. It was something new, and I was slowly falling in love with the little one. How could I not?

"You seem to be lost in thought today," Kelly said as she sat down across from me.

"Sorry," I said sheepishly as I fed Lilly. Kelly had said she enjoyed the break, as she was a demanding little thing while at home.

"Want to talk about it?" she asked, tilting her head to the side. She had her hair down today. She always looked perfectly put together despite the lack of care she said she took.

"I don't know where to start," I shrugged.

"At the beginning?" Kelly hinted. "That's usually the best place."

"Okay," I replied with a deep breath out. "I …. I didn't think I wanted anything sexual, as the whole time I was there under those men's watchful eyes, I didn't. I fought as much as I could. But I'm . . . *craving* . . . more with Elijah." I finished near a whisper. *Craving more* was only the tip of the list. I wasn't even sure he'd be willing to do anything with me, as we still hadn't figured out what *we* were.

"Oh Sug, it's totally normal. I'm guessing you haven't talked to Elijah about this?" she asked, with no hint of anger or malice.

"No!" I said, a little louder than intended. "There's no way

I can. He won't let me help him out as it is. We haven't really talked about our relationship, either."

"Well, this really should be something you talk to him about. I know he's told you time and time again he will always listen to you. He is attracted to you, always has been, and would be willing to help and understand your place in this. But you do know his tastes are not what most people call normal, right?"

"I know that," I said. "I'm not sure I can do what he wants." I looked up and met her eyes. I was sure my emotions were swimming in mine.

"Just talk to him. You'd be surprised what he could do, and he might even be willing to give up that lifestyle when it comes to you, if need be. He's good at what he does, or so I'm told. He knows you, and himself, so he would never push you into something you didn't want to do, Dawn."

"I'll try," I said, looking back down. "I don't think he'd be willing to give up something he's worked so hard at for me. I'm just . . . . me.

"That's all you have to be," she said with a smile.

∽

ELIJAH

A dream. It had to be. I was hard as a rock as a faceless woman lay on the bed with her head hanging off the side. Her eyes were closed, her dark hair touched the floor. Her warm mouth was open and waiting; her hands lay folded on her stomach, and her legs were bent and spread.

I entered her warm mouth slowly, teasing myself. I knew I wouldn't be able to hold on for long, so I wanted to prolong my release as much as possible. She moaned as she licked my tip, making my eyes roll back at the feeling.

I slowly pushed myself in, inch by inch, until I was fully sheathed by her warm heat. She sucked and ran her tongue on the upper side of my cock, initiating another loud moan from me.

Unable to take any more teasing, I began to pump into her mouth, a little faster after her throat relaxed to take more of me in. At this angle, everything felt tighter.

With one last push, I came, hard, and she swallowed everything with a loud moan.

I opened my eyes to a mostly darkened room, with Dawn smiling up at me from where she'd just sucked me off. Breathing hard, I flopped my head back down on the pillow.

"Dawn," I said huskily, more amazed that she didn't wake me up until now. I could tell she was pleased with herself. I ran my hands through her hair, where they'd somehow got tangled, down to her shoulders, where she only wore a tank top. I stopped my hands on the top of her arms, trying to wake my blissful brain up.

Finally, once my eyes gained focus, and my brain came back to earth, I pushed myself up and reached over to turn the bedside lamp on.

Meeting Dawn's green eyes, I could see she was proud of herself, but worried—most likely what my reaction would be. I wasn't sure if I should be upset at her for taking what she wanted, or to be pleased. Her light pink tank top showed her pointed nipples.

"Thank you, but why?" I asked, not yet deciding on what to do.

"You were moaning in your sleep," she replied, blushing, looking down and away from me. I lifted her chin, making her meet my eyes. I wasn't going to let her talk her way out of this one; I wanted to see how she felt.

"Hmmm," I replied, seeing what else she had to say. There was more.

"And you were hard . . ." she whispered, glancing up at me through her eyelashes.

"So you just decided to help?" I asked, half amused.

"Yes, Sir?" she said, more of a question. I could see the worry in her eyes.

"I see," I said, not giving anything away and keeping my face calm and relaxed. "And what do you expect out of that?"

"Um . . . to help you?" she asked, biting her lower lip. I was getting hard again, and she wasn't even doing anything.

"How do you think you should be dealt with?" I asked, watching as her eyes went wide, part in lust, and part in worry.

"However you see fit, Sir," she whispered, trying to look down again. I cleared my throat, making her look back at me.

"Well, I'm undecided," I replied, letting my other hand run down her arm.

I knew she was at that stage where she needed something —anything—from me for her release. I wasn't sure she knew how to please herself, but she was sure good at pleasing me. I'd been hoping she'd talk to me about this, but she did at least talk to Kelly, who called me on her way home today about Dawn's fears. I wasn't surprised in the least; I just didn't expect Dawn to try while I was sound asleep.

I'd thought I was clear that we'd talk about this next step when she felt ready. Apparently, she wasn't comfortable enough to talk to me about it, but ready all the same.

She didn't need to be punished for taking what she wanted. I could help bring her pleasure, showing her how to do it herself. There were a number of possibilities.

"What is it you want me to do?" I asked.

She looked shocked and confused before acceptance ghosted over her eyes.

"I don't want to be punished," she nearly whispered, her voice quivering.

"Then what do you want, my sweet girl?" I asked, running my thumb over her lips, not able to help myself.

I knew I was in love with this woman, who had captured my heart as a child.

"I'm not sure . . ." she said. "I just need . . ."

"You need something like you gave me? An orgasm?" I asked lightly.

She only nodded as her cheeks turned red.

"I can do that easily," I said with a smile. "But first, we need to talk."

"Okay?" she asked, confused.

"What do you want out of our relationship?" I asked.

"What normal people have," Dawn answered, her voice quiet and afraid I wouldn't agree.

"So, like a relationship?" I asked.

"Yes. I want what Kelly and Kaleb have," she answered, looking up at me for a moment.

"I see . . ." I trailed off, wondering how to go about this. "How much of what they have do you want?"

"I want to feel like I belong," she answered, averting her eyes from mine. "I want to feel normal."

"Being in a relationship won't make you feel normal. No one's normal these days," I hinted. "I don't want you to do something you may not be ready for, or even don't want."

"But I do want it!" she said, almost pleadingly. "I like you!"

"You like me?" I asked, trying to hide my surprise.

"I wouldn't have tried what I did if I didn't," she mumbled, a blush covering her cheeks.

"Alright," I said, suppressing my laugh. Now wasn't the time. "The list of things still applies; I still want your respect, and please tell me openly what you want or need from me."

"Okay," she said, surprised.

"So, I'll ask you again," I began. "What do you want from me? Am I your boyfriend, then?"

Dawn nodded her head, a silent yes.

"Out loud, please."

"Yes," she whispered.

"And do you still want me to help one of your cravings?"

"Yes, Sir. Please," she answered breathily.

"Okay, that I can do," I replied. "Go ahead and lie back."

She blinked, then moved to lie back down on her pillow. Her black hair splayed out around her head. Her eyes were filled with nervousness and hope.

"Let me know if you want me to stop, or if I'm hurting you in any way, Dawn," I said, before I began to touch her naked leg gently.

"Okay," she replied, wide-eyed. I'm sure she was surprised that I was going to allow her pleasure.

"As a Dom, it is my responsibility to make sure all your needs are met," I said, moving my hand up from her knee. "And that includes this need you feel right now."

Her cheeks were flushed, in both embarrassment and arousal. Swiping my fingers gently over her center, I found her underwear wet—almost soaked through.

"Are you wet for me?" I asked, keeping my eyes on her flushed face.

She moaned, closing her eyes as I put just a tad bit of pressure on her clit, and arching up, seeking more. I lay down beside her, not moving my hand.

"You *are* wet, aren't you, Dawn?" I asked, slipping my fingers under her panties. I was surprised she was so ready, and willing, after everything she'd been through.

"Yes, Sir," she said breathlessly.

I couldn't help but smile at the pleasure on her face. I slipped one of my fingers into her warmth and she instantly arched and moaned quietly. I was careful, and went slowly, adding two more fingers into her, one at a time.

"Do you like this? Me, bringing you pleasure?" I asked quietly, not wanting to break the mood by talking any louder. After a moment, when she didn't answer, I told her to speak.

"Y . . . yes Sir," she answered.

I found the spot that would bring the most pleasure to her, and gently rubbed against it as my palm put pressure against her clit. She was close, her moaning and panting increasing.

"Come for me, sweet girl'," I said, coaxing her to let it go. It was only a couple of seconds before she came, arching into my hand and panting hard. I could feel her heartbeat racing as I took my hand away. Her eyes slowly opened, and she had a smile on her face. She looked more relaxed than I had ever seen her.

"Feel better?" I smiled.

She simply nodded, gazing at me with awe, and something else I couldn't place.

"Come here," I said, pulling her to me, and gently kissing her on her lips. She was a sight to behold: warm green eyes and a happy smile.

She didn't kiss back, but I didn't expect her to. I pulled away after only a second, smiling down at her. "Let's get back to sleep. It's way too early to be starting the day."

"Okay," she said, snuggling into my side once she caught her breath. It didn't take long for her breathing to even out, and I followed shortly after.

CHAPTER 16

DAWN

I was laying partially on top of Elijah when I woke up. He had one hand on my hip, holding me to him. He was snoring slightly, still fast asleep. I was surprised I'd been able to bring him pleasure, expecting him to wake up before I ever got my mouth around him. I didn't even think he'd give pleasure in return, but he did.

His hands on me were amazing, and that kiss was even better. The only thing I didn't get trained in was kissing, since most men wouldn't even put their faces close to mine, or any of the girls, as we were constantly sick.

His kiss was gentle and sweet, the first of something I hoped there would be more of. His lips were soft, yet hard and so warm. I didn't know what to do; I was frozen. It was simple, but meant so much to me at the same time.

I knew I was slowly falling in love with him, and that wasn't a good thing. What would he do to me if he found out? Would he send me away? Ignore me again? I hoped that wouldn't happen, as I had grown closer to him more in this week than I had the past month.

All the stories of us growing up showed me how close we'd been once, and I wasn't sure if Elijah expected that of me now, since I wasn't the little girl I once was. I almost wished I'd gone to someone else, so I wouldn't feel such a pull to this man.

The sun was shining through the curtain that didn't get closed all the way. I had trouble sleeping most nights, so I'd taken to opening the curtains and watching the sky or the woods instead, since Elijah hadn't made his way to the bed often until this week.

I briefly glanced at the clock on his side of the bed. It was just after nine in the morning. I was surprised—I guessed the sleepless nights had finally caught up to me.

I was sure he was just as tired, if not more, since the past week he had been making sure he was up way before I ever was. Maybe after this morning, he would be more willing to stay and sleep in the bed with me.

I couldn't stop looking at him. He looked so relaxed as he slept. He looked younger than he was, and I had to wonder how long he was going to be taking off work.

"Enjoy staring at me?" he asked, opening his eyes in slits.

I blushed at being caught but didn't look away. I did like looking at him; he was easy on the eyes.

He groaned as his phone began to ring and he twisted to grab it.

"Hello?" he asked grouchily. I almost wanted to laugh at him but thought better of it.

Since I had to pee, I got up and used the bathroom, deciding to take a shower while I was in there, too. Once I was finished and dressed in my usual yoga pants and simple black top, I brushed my hair out, letting it air dry.

Once downstairs, I found Elijah waiting in the kitchen for me. A bowl of cereal sat at my normal place, and I took my seat. He stood behind me and began to braid my hair into a French braid off to the side.

"Thank you," I said. I loved it when he took the time to do my hair, even though it made it so he wasn't able to run his fingers through it as easily.

"My pleasure," he said with a warm smile.

Once I was done, he took my dishes away and put them in the dishwasher. He seemed half lost in thought, and I didn't want to ask, but had a feeling that it had something to do with the phone call. Instead, I just watched him, hoping he would at least let me know if it was about me or not. Most likely it was.

While Elijah went and made a few more phone calls, I did my normal housecleaning, which didn't take long. Not knowing what to do next, I looked through the cookbooks Joslyn had brought over, wanting to try to make some sort of cookies, hoping it would get my mind off Elijah and the mood he seemed to be in.

Plus, Kelly said the way to a man's' heart was through cooking.

Elijah stepped into the kitchen right as I put a sheet of cookies into the oven. He seemed worn out when I turned around.

"What kind of cookies are you making?" he asked, leaning up against the counter beside the oven.

"Peanut butter," I answered. "I wasn't sure what kind you liked best, and they were my favorite when I was younger."

"I remember," he said, watching me. "You loved almost any kind of cookies, though."

"Still do," I smiled, looking down at the floor for a moment. "I haven't had cookies for a long time."

"I'm glad you chose to make some," he replied, grabbing my hand and bringing me closer to him. I let him, meeting him half way as one hand came up to his chest. "Galvin called me." His voice was calm but sad.

"Oh?" I said, not sure what I was to say.

"He wants to see you," Elijah went on. "I've put it off for a number of reasons, the major one being that I don't want any of those men around you if I can do anything about it. But if I keep doing it, he'll know something is up and it could cost me my undercover job."

"I understand, Sir," I whispered. Really, I did. His job was on the line; I'd survive.

"I don't want to make you do this, but you will have to show Galvin that you serve me, and only me. I won't let him touch you in any way, but you will have to be in the same room for just a few minutes. I called Kaleb, and he will be close by in case anything happens, but I don't think it will. We don't plan to arrest Galvin until last, so we can get some of the men that would be taking over his place in situations such as these."

I wanted to reach out and let him know that I would be okay—that I understood—but I didn't know *how*. I wasn't used to trying to soothe someone else, and the feelings scared me.

"I have a soft pillow by my office chair that you will kneel on. I won't purposely ignore you, but I have to act a part, so please don't be upset about anything I say, or how I say it. I will touch you to give you comfort, but nothing in punishment or sexual. Okay?" he continued, hugging me tight to him.

"Okay," I said, but it came out mumbled as my face was pressed into his warm chest.

"I want you to ignore him as best as you can, along with anyone he brings with him. I don't expect him to come alone, I just don't know who he will bring with him, but I will do my best to keep you safe. I will try to get you out of the room after a few moments after Galvin has whatever he wants from me. When I dismiss you, you will need to go to the spare room, as I don't want him thinking I view you as an equal," he said. "I hate having to make you do any of this. I hope you understand I hate myself for even asking you to pretend to be my slave. You are nothing like that."

"I'll be okay, Elijah," I said, looking up at him. His eyes softened, and he kissed me on my forehead as the oven buzzed.

I set the cookie pan on the stove, letting them cool before plating them and wrapping them in tin foil. They'd hopefully make a treat for the men, although I hated the idea of it. I kept my emotions under control, trying to show Elijah I would be okay. I was nervous and scared, but I could do this. I had to for him.

As the doorbell rang, Elijah told me to wait in his office, and I did as I was told while he answered the door. I found the soft pillow easily and knelt on it. Elijah hadn't told me the complete position to wait in; I kept my knees together, hands folded in front of me and my head down. At that time, I wished I had my hair down to keep my face hidden from view of the men that had shown up. My stomach was in knots.

It wasn't a full two minutes before Elijah led the men—at least three—towards the office. I kept my head down as they all entered. He stroked my head as he headed to his chair. I heard the three others take their seats but kept still. I felt a tinge of calm with his touch.

"What I can I do for your gentlemen today?" Elijah asked, brushing his foot up against my knees.

"I haven't seen you at the warehouse the past few weeks, and I was concerned. It's not like you," I heard Calvin answer. His voice was still high-pitched and make me want to shiver and hide away as far as I could.

"Sorry about that," Elijah replied, not missing a beat. "I've been trying to tie up loose ends with that investigation, as they were getting too close on a few things."

"Ah yes, you have been a wonderful help on that front," Galvin laughed lightly. "I hope you got all of us cleared?"

"Yes, I have. My 'boss' thinks I was stressed, so he took me off, but not before I got a few things taken care of so nothing is traced back to any of us," Elijah said, leaning back in his chair, acting relaxed.

"I'm sure you're enjoying your purchase?" Galvin asked.

"Absolutely," Elijah replied in a smile.

"Trained to your liking?" Galvin, again.

"For the most part," Elijah said. "A few things that needed to be fixed to my liking, but nothing I couldn't handle."

"Your family maid has been here a lot," Morgan said. I jumped, not expecting him to be here, but got my fear under control.

"I hired someone to teach her to cook properly," Elijah said tensely. "I refuse to cook if I have someone able to do so easily."

"Home cooked meals are wonderful indeed," Galvin agreed. "How is the cooking?"

"Lovely," Elijah said. "Dawn, please get our guests those cookies you made earlier," he said, turning to me.

"Yes, Sir," I said, standing up. I was more than happy to escape for a moment, even if for only a moment.

I ignored the men as I left the office, taking my time to get the plate of cookies. I took a few deep breaths and a couple sips of water before turning around to grab the plate. I stopped as I heard heavy footsteps enter the kitchen. I froze, knowing right away it wasn't the man I was slowly falling in love with.

"Well hello, pet," the man sneered as he took another step towards me. I slowly turned around, keeping my eyes down to the floor, hoping I wouldn't have to see Erick's face. I never liked him, and would never be what he wanted me to be. "Aren't you going to give me a greeting?"

I ignored him, but took a step to the side, hoping I could

get around him and to the safety of my 'room', and that Elijah would figure out where I was and not worry about me.

"Oh, no you don't," Erick laughed, moving over and towards me, caging me in against the counter. My heart began to beat faster, but I did my best to keep my panic at bay, at least until he'd either leave or Elijah came to find me before anything happened.

"Erick?" Morgan called as he entered the kitchen. "Galvin wants you back in the office."

"Yeah, yeah. Give me a minute, Morgan," Erick replied, brushing the demand away as he stared at me. He was now close enough to touch me, and I pushed myself back into the countertop as much as I could. I wanted to be invisible.

"Oh, I see why," Morgan laughed as he entered the kitchen.

"She was to be mine, but Galvin just had to sell her," Erick seethed, turning his head to look at Morgan, but keeping me in his line of sight.

"You know Galvin has his plans and reasons," Morgan said calmly as he moved up next to me. "I will get her back to her mother soon, and then you can have your share of her."

"Ah, yes. How is that working out for you? I hear Eli is of no help," Erick laughed, bringing a hand to my upper arm. I flinched, making him laugh. He squeezed me harder, giving a look that clearly told me not to make a sound.

"I have Hughes working on it for me. Can you believe how easy it is to do something like this right under the fed's noses?" Morgan laughed, bringing his hand up my other arm. I wanted to scream, to run, but my body was frozen.

"I can't wait till I can play," Erick laughed, leaning in to smell my hair. I couldn't stop the cringe I made, making him laugh more.

"That's my property you're both touching," Elijah hissed. I didn't hear him come in but was relieved he'd finally showed up. Morgan and Erick instantly backed off. I was still frozen in my spot. After a moment, Elijah said my name, and I went to him with panic on the edge. I wanted nothing but to run to him—to my safety.

Instead, I slowly walked to him on shaky legs. He pulled me to him, and I breathed in his scent, not being able to help the few tears that leaked out my eyes. Somehow, he was just able to make me feel okay with his presence alone.

"What made you think you could touch his pet?" Galvin said calmly.

"She's a slut; she's been made to let any man touch her, and she will never be what he wants," Erick replied. "I marked her, and she can never have a normal life, so I don't see what the harm is."

"When I step back from you, you need to go upstairs, and don't look back," Elijah whispered in my ear. "I need you to hide in the closet, and lock the door behind you."

"She's not yours, Erick!" Galvin nearly shouted, outraged. "You have not been a follower, but doing your own thing. That is why I didn't permit you to have her!"

I felt Elijah's phone vibrate against my hip, and he kissed the top of my head before whispering, "Now."

I looked up at him briefly before walking away hurriedly up the stairs to the closet. I made sure to close the door softly, turning the lock as quickly as I could. I didn't think anyone followed, but I still had to follow orders.

I found two pillows, a battery-operated lantern, and a blanket folded neatly in the corner. I had to wonder if Elijah had expected something like to this happen. He most likely did, as he seemed to be prepared for just about anything.

I couldn't hear anything from the men, but that was probably good, as my panic was already setting in. My heartbeat was loud, my palms sweaty. I was worried about Elijah, and if I was safe hiding here.

Taking a pillow and hugging it to my chest, I backed into the far corner where the items were, hoping to find some sort of calm there, even though it was unlikely to happen. I wanted my Elijah. I ended up closing my eyes and rocking back and forth as I full out panicked.

~

I COULD HEAR LAUGHING AS MY ARMS WERE TIED IN FRONT OF ME *and my legs were held down. There was an audience at the door and I refused to give them any of my time. I breathed in and out, trying to picture myself anywhere but here.*

"It's almost over, sweetie pie," Morgan groaned as he pounded into me roughly. "Daddy likes you tight and wet, just for me." I gagged at the name.

This wasn't the first time, nor would it be the last. I wanted to pass out so I could have the darkness instead of the pain. Instead, I just lay there, limply, hoping it would all end. Either I could pass out, Morgan finishing quickly so I could be thrown back into my cell, or just die.

"That's how Daddy likes it," he grunted as he froze on top of me. After a few moments, he pulled out and shooed the bystanders off.

Afterward, he was gentle, picking me up and carrying me back to my cell, where he tenderly cleaned me up. He told me how he loved me, how he couldn't wait for my mother to be out of the picture like my father, so he could be the one to take care of me. Morgan wanted me to keep his needs met twenty-four seven. I couldn't stop the tears, knowing what he wanted wasn't right.

I couldn't help but remember another time in that place.

"Please," I cried out, holding my torso as the pain racked through my veins. My ribs hurt and it hurt to breathe. Galvin stood by, watching as Morgan and another man I didn't know took turns kicking and hitting me—all because I refused to let two men use my body at one time. I knew I shouldn't have fought, but I had to. I had that small amount of hope flare up that I may be saved from this hell.

"Cry some more," Galvin laughed. "It's like music to my ears, dear one."

With another kick, I blacked out, letting the promising darkness take over. I hoped I wouldn't wake up this time.

The memories faded and I lifted my head, my vision blurry as I grabbed the pillow and hugged it. It smelt like Elijah's laundry soap, but not like him.

I wanted Elijah.

I wanted out.

CHAPTER 17

ELIJAH

I was seething inside. It took everything in me to not pound my fist into their faces. Erick was smug, able to get one up on me and touching what didn't belong to him. I knew he would try to do something.

Morgan at least had the decency to look ashamed. I knew he wanted more than any man should from Dawn, but at least he'd tried to not keep looking at her while all of us were in my office. Erick, on the other hand, couldn't keep his eyes off her—or his thoughts, I'm sure.

I knew something was going to happen when Erick said he needed to answer a phone call, as did Galvin, and he sent Morgan out just a few seconds later.

I didn't want these men in my house, but there wasn't anything I could do about it if I didn't want any questions asked about what I was really up to. Dawn had taken the news well, surprisingly. I didn't expect her to be so calm. At the same time, it was who she was trained to be by these men. I could tell she had shut down, closing off her emotions.

I hated seeing her having to do that, but understood why: it was her way of protecting herself. I quickly shot a text off to Kaleb, letting him go ahead with our plan while I followed Galvin to the kitchen. He wasn't happy, either.

I didn't want to let Dawn go, but I wasn't sure what would happen to her if she was close when Kaleb showed up. All our planning was shot out the window, but we'd make it work to the best of our ability.

Knowing Mike had been taken into custody this morning after trying to find something in Kaleb's office hadn't helped my sour attitude after Galvin had called.

I sadly watched her hurry away like her tail was on fire. I knew she'd be safe, as long as she did what I told her. It was the closest place to keep her safe—for the time being.

"Sorry about these two," Galvin said, turning back to me. "They both know better than to touch what doesn't belong to them."

"She belongs to me," Erick said with a glare as he walked past me. "She's a slut. I enjoyed taking her that first time, and I will take her again and again once I get my hands on her."

I couldn't stop my reaction. I turned around and punched him in the face. The sound of my fist hitting his jaw echoed around the kitchen. He also got couple punches in before Morgan pulled him back. My cheek stung like a motherfucker.

"Boys, boys, boys," Galvin said, shaking his head. "Erick, I will deal with you when we get back to the compound. Morgan, you may go wait in the car."

Morgan left, not saying anything, but I knew he was looking around the house. He had something up his sleeve—I just wasn't sure what.

"Now, Erick, please apologize to Mr. Hunter, since you were threatening his property. We've had this talk before," Galvin said in his high-pitched voice, sounding bored.

"Sorry, Mr. Hunter," Erick mumbled, looking anywhere

but at me. He would have a few sore bruises, as I got more hits in on him.

"Now, back to why we are here today," Galvin said, taking a cookie off the abandoned plate. "She's done well, cooking wise."

"She's a fast learner," I said. "I was glad to see she was able to have some learning tools to help her do her job here."

"All the girls are required to have some knowledge of reading and writing, since most are meant to cook meals. That's why I have an age limit. Normally, I don't take ones so young, but due to her mother's . . . . debts, I didn't have a choice," Galvin said sadly. "I'm glad she is doing well here."

Dawn had taken well to the change, better than I would have expected. She wasn't as skittish as many girls would have been after living in such an abusive situation.

"She's just what I needed," I said.

"Perfect," Galvin said. I could faintly hear two cars coming up the driveway, but only because I knew they were coming. "Are you by chance interested in another? I have another auction coming up in a week."

"Possibly. Where will it be? The same place?" I asked, taking a stand against the counter to make it seem like I was calm. It would be perfect to get men in that building and get those girls out after these men were taken to jail.

"As it always is," Erick mumbled.

"Hush, boy," Galvin said, giving Erick a look. I could tell Erick wanted to be anywhere but under the watchful of this man. I didn't blame him, really. Galvin was full of power and could end his life easily without a thought.

"I didn't do anything!" Erick said, agitated, flinging his hands up.

At that moment, Kaleb and two officers came barging into the kitchen, yelling, "hands up!" I instantly put my hands up, watching as Erick and Galvin were handcuffed behind their backs and told their rights. I made sure to keep my face in a state of shock.

"Where's Dawn?" Kaleb asked once he got the two men into the police cars, saying he needed my statement. He already had my view of what went down, since it was mostly completely planned out.

"Upstairs, hopefully not panicking. Did you get Morgan?" I answered, walking away to go find my girl, knowing he'd follow.

"No, he must have left as soon as he went out, but at least we got those two. The others will fall in easily, and we have a team at the compound as we speak getting most of the other men," Kaleb said.

"He'll show back up here, and probably with Joan," I sighed, not sure how I would deal with that. Morgan already left a threat on my voice mail about doing anything to get to Dawn. I of course, told my FBI team about it.

Getting to the closet after unlocking the door, I saw my girl hugging a pillow tightly to her chest. "Dawn?" She was rocking back and forth, her arms wrapped around a pillow, her knees pulled up as tight as they could be.

"Dawn?" I repeated, easing my way into the room, hoping not to scare her. I called her name louder, and she finally looked up at me with wide red eyes.

"Elijah?" she whispered, but seemed confused.

"Come here, sweetheart," I coaxed. She began to slowly move, still not quite herself, as the panic was still full force.

"Will you be okay if I leave? I have to be back at the office to oversee the ones that will be brought in shortly," Kaleb said once I had Dawn in my arms.

"That's my girl," I said to her, before nodding at Kaleb. "I'll be fine. Make sure the doors are locked before you leave, please."

"Of course, brother," he nodded before leaving me.

"Dawn?" I asked again. She still seemed to be in a daze.

What was she thinking, or remembering, in the short time that she was in that room? "Can you talk to me?"

"Elijah," she said again as she laid her head on my shoulder.

"I'm sorry I had you go in there, but it was safer. Galvin and Erick won't ever hurt you again," I said, hoping my voice would bring her back from her thoughts. "Morgan ran off before Kaleb and his fellow officers got here."

I had never seen her like this, but I knew whatever she was remembering had to be worse than her dreams that she'd woken up from many nights in a row. I just knew that she wasn't truly with me, as her eyes were glazed over in a dazed-like panic state.

I gently picked her up and carried her to the bed, where I tried to lay her down, but she only hung on as tight as she possibly could, and her breathing picked up. Not wanting to cause her more panic, I easily slid onto the bed with her wrapped around me.

I somehow maneuvered a blanket from the end of the bed up around Dawn's shoulders, to help with the shaking that was wracking her body. I was at a loss of what to do for her, other than hold her and comfort her. I slowly ran my fingers through her hair while I talked to her.

"You've done wonderfully today," I soothed quietly. "I am so proud of you."

I leaned back against the headboard and pillows with Dawn curled up in my lap and her head on my shoulder. Her knees were still pulled up to her chest, but at least her breathing began to even out some.

Looking down at her, I saw her eyes were closed, but her face was still saddened with worry and fear, even as she slept. My heart hurt, knowing I couldn't do anything about it right now.

CHAPTER 18

DAWN

*V*oices fluttered in and out, but none of them reached my ears as I lay in a fetal position on the bed. I hardly moved, hardly slept. Every time I closed my eyes, my past bombarded me. It wouldn't go away. It left me breathless. I had no hope left.

"Dawn, sweetie, please," I heard Emily beg as she kneeled in front of me. Her eyes were rimmed in red like she'd been crying.

I simply blinked at her, not able to do anything else. My brain was like mush or turned off. It wouldn't think, wouldn't let me move.

I don't know how long she stayed before I felt Elijah pull me to him, hugging me and holding me. He whispered soothing words, calming whatever was going on in my mind. I felt out of control—lost. I wanted to be found and brought out of my head, but it seemed pointless.

I could feel the man on top of me, but I couldn't see his face as my eyes were swollen shut. I was worried I may suffer some head injury from when Erick had slammed it into the floor just the day before. I had fought him, again, and had to pay the price for doing so.

The man grunted as he sped up. I couldn't feel him; he was as small as my pinky. I didn't mind. As least it was an easy chore. It didn't take much from me as I lay there limply. I just wanted to go to sleep, but Morgan kept coming in and waking me up, or dragging me to another client.

This current guy seemed concerned for me, though. He wasn't the first, and probably wouldn't be the last. He was gentler, even though I thought this was the first time he'd come here.

It didn't take him long to finish and leave me at peace for a moment. I let the darkness consume me, for just a few minutes, before Morgan came and lifted me up. I groaned, not wanting to move as he forced me to my feet once again.

"Let her mind come to terms with things, son," I heard Vence talk from the doorway. "She won't eat, so any meds I could possibly prescribe won't be able to help without food in her system." His voice was quiet, but I could hear the hint of worry in it.

"Is there anything I can do to help her?" Elijah asked.

"Just be there for her. You will most likely have to force her to eat and drink today. She can't go on much longer without anything, since she's still so underweight."

"Time to wake up, child," Galvin said happily as he banged the door open.

I groggily opened my eyes, squinting against the light from the hallway. I had been in my cell in complete darkness again as a punishment for not obeying.

"Up you get," Galvin demanded as he stood above me, looking down at me in disgust. "You have a client waiting."

Slowly and shakily, I lifted myself up. My arms could hardly support my weight as I pushed myself up. My legs weren't any better. Once standing, I slowly followed Master Galvin out into the hallway. I wasn't sure where we were going, as he had never been the one to lead me to my next hellhole. He loved to watch the men take me and other countless girls.

Going down a different hallway, loud rap music reached my ears. It was noisier this way, but just as filthy as any other part of this prison.

"Now, this is a special client, so you'd better not disappoint me. He paid a good penny to spend his time here tonight with just you," Galvin said, motioning to an open room with a door posted on its hinges. "I expect you to be on your best behavior, understood?"

"Yes Sir," I answered, keeping my head down.

Once I was in the room, just like all the others, but with a small bowl of condoms on the table, I made my way to the bed, where I was sure I'd have to lie by command.

"Hello, my dear," said the man in a calm and friendly tone. I kept my head down as I took a seat on the edge of the bed, waiting for instructions.

"Hello, Sir," I answered politely, my voice just above a whisper.

"Look at me," he said. I slowly looked up at him. He was familiar, but I wasn't sure why. Maybe he had rented me before, but his voice didn't seem like one I had heard here yet. He smiled and took a seat next to me as the door shut, closing us in.

"I won't hurt you," he said gently, making sure he wasn't touching me in any way. His light hazel eyes shone with compassion. He was bigger, filled with muscle and strength. His round face was shadowed in worry, but also a sort of calm. I couldn't tell what his hair was like, since he wore a beanie down to his ears. His clothes were simple, jeans and shirt.

"I don't really want anything but your time, and maybe a little information about you," he continued. "I just want to give you a break from having to do what others want you to do."

I was confused, and it must have shown on my face. Why would he waste his time, and money, to just spend it with me, talking of all things?

BROKEN REVIVAL

"I have been here before, just keeping an eye on things to make sure no one was killed while they pleased the men," he said quietly. "I've seen you a few times, usually with more bruises than the rest of the girls here—and you're so much thinner than the rest, too."

"Oh," I said. That made sense, I guess.

"How long have you been here?" he asked.

"I'm not sure, Sir," I answered. I had no idea how long I had been held here. Maybe a year? Two years?

"Hmm," he said, thinking. "It's 2013, mid-March."

"So, about a year and a half then, Sir," I answered.

"That long?" he said, shocked and leaning back on his hands.

I shrugged, not having anything to say to that. I had no choice in the matter.

"Why are you here, girl?" he asked. "Being so young, you aren't the type or age Galvin usually brings in."

"I don't know, Sir. Morgan brought me here to pay a debt off for my mother," I simply answered. That was the only answer I ever got when I had the courage to ask.

"Where is your mother, then? Shouldn't she be the one paying the debt off, not you?" he asked, cocking his head to the side and watching me with his light hazel eyes.

"I don't know. Somewhere better than here," I answered.

"So, you aren't here willingly?" the man asked, looking at me, almost through me, in a way.

I shook my head. "I don't think anyone is here willingly. Not with what we are forced to endure."

"I see," he said. "I'm guessing you don't know when you'll be allowed to leave, then?"

"No, Sir," I answered sadly. I wished I knew. I wished I wasn't here now. I would gladly even take my father's place than be here.

"I'll see what I can do to get you out. I'll talk to Galvin, but I highly doubt he'd let you go willingly—not yet. He seems to like you," he said. "Oh, by the way, I'm Kevin."

He left shortly afterward, claiming I was the best action he'd had in months, with the promise of wanting my services again. I never did see him again after that, but I didn't think much of it, either. What would be the point? So many men came and went, and I hardly ever remembered names after the deed was done.

The next day, Joslyn came by, and with the help of Elijah, I was made to take a bath. It felt nice to be clean, but I still didn't want to face reality. I didn't want to face my nightmares. I wanted to be in between the past and the present—or skip to the future, if it were possible.

After being bathed and dressed in clean clothes, Elijah fed me spoonful after spoonful of soup, in a tender and loving manner. I was sure I looked like a wreck, but he never said anything; never demanded me to come out of the space my brain was in. He could have, and I would have followed his orders.

Time seemed to become a blur once again, the nightmares and what was real crashing into one another. I woke a few times, gasping for breath. Each time, Elijah was there, holding me, talking me down and calming my racing heart. I just wanted it to end.

I briefly thought about how easy it would be to end my life then. Elijah never once left me alone, but I could have used the razor blades in the bathroom, or starved myself to death. It wouldn't take much. I had nothing to live for, no reason to keep on fighting the darkness that weighed heavily on my shoulders.

Emily was currently sitting in the rocking chair, reading a magazine, making comments here and there, but I mostly tuned her out. I wanted to sleep, but sleep was not coming easily for me, once again. Elijah was up here about an hour before, making sure I ate some food on my own this time. He said it was progress.

Emily had tried to talk to me about therapy, and how it was helping her cope with what she went through, but it seemed to go in one ear and out the other. I had no reason to listen. It wouldn't help me.

The doorbell rang, and I figured it was Joslyn and Vence again. With a sigh, I closed my eyes, hoping sleep would give me some peace of mind.

CHAPTER 19

ELIJAH

I couldn't believe it. He really had the nerve to show up here again, and so soon. Morgan stood at my door, hand poised to ring the doorbell. He looked worn down and dirty. I did have to wonder what he had been up to the past week.

Behind him stood Joan, holding a shoe box that had some sort of blanket sticking out underneath the lid. She didn't look happy as she glared past me. Her blond hair was hastily pulled back in a bun. She had aged years in just a short time. I was glad Dawn was upstairs with Emily.

Dawn had been distant, as much as she had when she first came here, if not more. I was worried about her. She would hardly talk to me, but I knew she was listening to everything I told her. Since Emily had been going to therapy, she was able to connect a little better with my girl and was more than willing to come by today to talk to her, even maybe get her to agree to start therapy to help with coping with what she had gone through.

"What can I do for you, Morgan?" I asked, setting my foot on my side of the door so he couldn't barge in.

"I can't deal with this *thing* Galvin left in my charge any longer," he answered, pointing at the box, his voice filled with distaste. "I didn't want it to begin with, but I couldn't let Erick or the others just throw it away, either."

"What it is?" I asked, keeping my expression hard. I wasn't sure I really wanted to know.

"Can we come in?" Morgan asked, almost ashamed about asking for my help. "It's cold, and this thing really can't be out in this weather."

The air was frigid with the incoming snow storm; the sky was covered in dark clouds with the wind beginning to rise in speed.

"Fine," I sighed, keeping the doubt out of my voice. What could he possibly have in there? I stepped out of the way, opened the door, and motioned towards my office. I shot a text off to Emily, to let her know to keep Dawn upstairs as her mother had shown up. That was not something my sweet girl needed to face just yet.

"Thank you," Joan said, taking a seat after placing the box on my desk—a lot softer than I would have expected. "And thank you for getting that picture of Dawn to me. She looked happy."

"Not a problem," I replied. I wanted to put that picture as my screensaver but knew I couldn't yet without possibly raising suspicion.

"When can I see her? Galvin was taken to jail, so isn't it safe now?" she asked.

I took a moment to look her over. The last time I saw her, she was upset and panicky. Now, she was calm, if not a little rattled at the same time. Her eyes were red, from both crying and tiredness, but there was acceptance at the same time.

"I'm not sure," I said truthfully. "Right now, it really is up to her, but she's going through a difficult time due to a scare she had a few days ago. She isn't talking to anyone, will hardly even let her new trusted friend be in the same room as her." That was an understatement. She wouldn't let Kaleb near her at all, and I could hardly get one word out of her.

"So, you do know where she is?" Joan asked, sitting up straighter.

"Yes," I said but didn't give anything else away.

"Where?" she asked, looking around the office for any sign of her.

"That's also up to her to decide. She knows a few things about what caused her to be in such conditions as she was in. She's nineteen, so it's completely her choice," I answered. Kaleb and Zack had come up with the idea of her deciding on what was best. We had talked to Dawn, or at least tried to, and got no reaction out of her one way or the other. I knew she didn't want to go with her mother if given the choice, and with her state right now, there was not any way I was going to let her.

"What do you mean?" Joan asked, standing up, her voice higher than necessary.

"Joan, calm down," Morgan sighed. "It's none of our concern."

"Don't you dare tell me to calm down," she seethed, glaring at Morgan.

"Hey, can you please keep it down," Emily said as she entered the office, glaring at the two. I was just about to tell them myself, but looking Emily's way, I could tell something was wrong.

"Emily?" I said, going to her so we could talk quietly, without the two guests hearing. I could hear Morgan mutter something underneath his breath about my soon to be sister-in-law.

"She won't calm down. I swear, I didn't do anything," she said quietly. That's when I noticed Dawn standing off towards the wall that kept her out of view of the office. I was surprised I hadn't felt her there. I guess I wasn't entirely paying attention, thinking she'd stay upstairs. "She heard voices . . ."

"It's okay, Emily," I said, laying a hand her shoulder. "Sweetheart?" I called my girl.

Her eyes were back to dull green, like she had given up. Her hair was a mess, as she kept grabbing it in handfuls, yanking it. She wore one of my sweatshirts, which was huge on her but looked good at the same time, along with pink yoga pants.

"Excuse me for a moment," I said to the two, who were still half arguing. I stepped away from the office towards where my sad girl stood, looking down at the floor.

"Hey," I said gently, lifting her chin up slightly with my index finger. She still refused to meet my eyes, looking past me. "What's going on in that mind of yours?"

I didn't expect an answer. I tilted my head, trying to meet her sad eyes. She still refused to look at me, but a tear leaked out. I didn't hesitate to bring her to me, wrapping my arms around her and laying my cheek against the top of her head.

"What were you talking about that made her upset?" I asked, turning to Emily, ignoring the raised voices in the office and Dawn stiffened more than she already was.

"I left the door open a crack, since having it closed all the way makes her panic, and we heard their voices. I tried to get her to stay, but she came down here, and I had to follow; I didn't know what else to do," Emily said, near tears herself.

"It's okay," I smiled gently. "Can you call Kaleb for me, please?"

"Yeah, sure," she said, taking a deep breath, and headed back upstairs. I knew Kaleb would want to know who was here, and if I could keep them longer, he could get someone here, along with himself.

"Dawn?" I said, hoping I got her attention. Her breathing was faster than normal, but not quite panic-fast yet. "I'm sure you know who's in my office right now. It's completely up to you, but you can either come in and face the music, or go back upstairs where Emily is, where you won't have to see them."

"Please," she mumbled out in a whisper, turning her face in my shoulder and neck. She tried to crawl into me.

"Okay," I said, taking a deep breath. "I won't let either of them take you from me. Ever."

"If it wasn't for your stupid ass, I wouldn't have had to sell my daughter!" Joan shouted, making Dawn jump and whimper into me.

"I wasn't the one who made you decide to become a drug addict," Morgan shot back. "And I didn't make you sell her. I only gave you the option!"

"Hey, enough," I hollered at them as I walked back into the room. I guess we had our answer now whether Joan knew what had happened.

I held Dawn against me with her back to the two, and her head turned into my shoulder. I felt her shaking and only pulled her closer in response. "Now, what was so important that you had to come by today, of all days? I do have things to do."

"It's in the box," Morgan said, motioning and glaring at the box that still sat on my desk. Joan huffed in response but stayed quiet as she slumped in the chair.

I slowly reached for the box. The lid had a few holes cut into the top. It was about the size of my shoe, which could be filled with just about anything. There was a weighted object inside of it.

Glancing first at my girl, who was still hiding behind me while her hands were wrapped around my left arm, then looking up at the two, who were both looking my way, I slowly lifted the lid up. I wasn't sure what I'd expected, but it sure wasn't the little thing wrapped up tightly in a blanket. She was tiny but looked healthy at first glance.

"A baby?" I asked, shocked, looking up at the two, and making Dawn glance up at me as she held her breath.

"One of the girls gave birth, and Galvin wanted me to 'take care of it'. I couldn't kill it. I already had to watch one girl lose a baby," Morgan said.

"I can't stand the crying of that *thing*," Joan said, crossing her arms over her chest.

"You can't stand anyone, no matter who they are these days," Morgan mumbled towards Joan.

"How dare you," Joan replied angrily. "I'm upset, you idiot. I want my daughter back. She was stolen from me."

"Joan, please," Morgan said. "You know she wasn't, now please knock it off."

"I will take her myself if I knew where she was," Joan seethed.

"How old is the baby?" I asked, touching her warm cheek, mostly to make sure she was alive and real.

"Less than a week," Morgan said. "The girl was only about seven or so months along, I think. I had her taken out of the compound so Erick didn't end it the same way as the last one, but she didn't survive the birth."

"Okay," I said, but then turned to Dawn. "Sweetie, I need my other hand. "

Her eyes were wide, but clearer, as she moved slightly back, keeping her back to the two who had put her into the life she hadn't wanted. Smiling down at her, I turned to the baby in the box. I gently picked it up, guessing it was less than five pounds. After laying it on the desk and unwrapping the blanket, I found no clothing, just a diaper that seemed full and in need of a change.

"Can you get me a diaper from the stash Kelly leaves here?" I asked, turning to Dawn, who was staring in frightened awe. She nodded and went to the living room.

"How old was the mother?" I asked, looking up at Morgan, who was now standing on the other side of the desk.

"Eighteen, or so," Morgan shrugged. "I really don't know. She was homeless, and Erick was in charge while she was at the compound, but she was pregnant before him, I think. I snuck her out when there weren't many guards, and took her to my place."

"Thanks," I said, taking the diaper and wipes from Dawn.

Changing the diaper, I saw the baby was indeed a girl, and was already thinking of what documents I would need and what phone calls to make.

"I'm sorry, child, for the other day," Morgan said, making Dawn jump. She was standing facing me, looking at the floor.

"What did you do now?" Joan huffed, coming to stand next to him with her arms folded across her chest.

I now had the baby wrapped back up, and was holding her in my arm, hoping Emily would be back so I could have her take the baby out of harm's way and call my dad to get here as soon as he could.

"He scared my girl," I said, nodding to Dawn as she grabbed onto me once again, but touching the baby at the same time. "Do you want to take her and go upstairs?"

She shook her head and shrugged. She was torn on what to do; stay with me, her safe place, or take this baby that was born into a world no one should have had to be away.

"Who is she, anyway?" Joan spat. "Just a waste of space. Both of them are."

"Joan," Morgan warned, right as Dawn glanced up at her. Dawn had tears in her eyes, but also determination and acceptance.

"What?" she glared at him, before moving her eyes my way. They widened in shock as they landed on Dawn.

"Elijah," Emily said, coming back into the room but stopping short when she saw what I was holding and the expressions on all our faces. She only paused for a moment, before turning to me and taking the baby, saying something about calling her father-in-law.

With both hands-free, I touched Dawn to get her attention. She turned around, and tears were falling from her eyes. She looked devastated.

"How?" Joan asked, shocked and pale.

"Dawn?" I said in her ear, "I think you should go back upstairs."

She shook her head, gripping my shirt. How could she not want to run from here?

"Okay. You can leave at any time," I said quietly. I turned back to Joan. "This is why she hasn't contacted you. It's been up to her from the start. I won't ever force her to do something she doesn't want to do."

"She's a minor; she has no choice," Joan said. "She will be going home with me now."

"She's nineteen, and even the courts can't force her to go with you if she chooses not to," Kaleb said as he entered the room, two police officers following him.

"You can't stop me taking her back," Joan said, while Morgan slowly backed up, trying to make himself invisible. "She's my daughter, for crying out loud! I have plans for her. She owes me for her worthless father."

"Sorry Ma'am, but you are both under arrest for child trafficking. Anything you say can and will be used against you in a court of law," Kaleb said, indicating to the two officers to arrest them.

Joan did not go quietly, giving away her plot of how she was going to get out and come for her daughter, who was meant to die, and telling us how Morgan had just killed a woman in her home. I pulled Dawn closer to me as Joan was dragged out, kicking and screaming. Morgan went willingly, accepting his fate, head down and tail between his legs.

"Are you okay, sweets?" Kaleb asked Dawn, who was shaking and suppressing her sobs against my chest. I knew Kaleb viewed my girl as a little sister and cared deeply about her.

"She will be," I said, hoping that was the truth.

"Alright. Give me a call later?" he asked, starting to leave.

"Sure, but you need to know, I need some things taken care of. Morgan and Joan brought a baby here, less than a week old." I said, rubbing my hand up and down Dawn's back as she took in some deep breaths, trying to get her crying to stop.

"What? Really?"

"Yeah. He said the mother didn't make it; Emily has her upstairs right now," I replied. "For the time being, I'd like the baby to stay here—after my dad checks her over, of course. She's a tiny thing."

"Of course," Kaleb said, not asking why. I wasn't even sure why I wanted the baby to stay, as I knew Emily would be more than happy to keep it as her own, if given the choice. With it being the one thing that really got my girl's attention, I couldn't just leave it in someone else's hands.

"Doc is on the way," Emily said, coming back in, holding the sleeping baby. "I called him and he should be here shortly."

"Thanks, Emily," I said gratefully. She really had been wonderful help this week, with not just Dawn, but everything.

"Not a problem," she answered, handing the baby over to Kaleb.

Taking a seat in the chair, Kaleb spoke, "Did Morgan say who her mother was?"

"No," I answered, taking a seat myself while Emily excused herself to wait for my father to arrive, and most likely my mother. By now, Dawn's sobbing was down to just a few sniffles and she was much calmer. She sat on my lap with her head on my shoulder. I was coming to think that was her favorite spot.

"Wonder if it was that young girl we found in an abandoned house a few days ago. The timing and blood loss would all match up," Kaleb mused. "It's hard to tell without DNA. I'm sure you want to keep this on the down-low?"

"If at all possible, yes."

My father arrived not long afterward, my mother in tow. Dawn hardly moved from her spot, but I could tell she was listening very closely to as much as she could hear. I gently shooed her off my lap so I could watch my father as he looked at the baby girl, and took any necessary pictures. Dawn stood close by with her hands in front of her. She was nervous, but I wasn't sure if it was for herself, or for the baby.

"Hello," my dad said, looking at Dawn before everyone else, and then turning his attention back to the baby who Kaleb had laid on the desk. "Less than a week old? Maybe about two, three days, at the most."

"Should she be monitored at all?" Emily asked, stepping closer to the baby.

"Strong heartbeat, good coloring, but very tiny," Vence said. "I don't think hospitalization is mandatory, but you do need to keep an eye on her for any breathing trouble, or anything not typical for a baby. Since she is preemie, she may be up more at night to eat, and lag behind most babies her age," he said, as he bundled the baby back up. He handed her to me. "What do you plan to do with her?"

"Keep her tonight, but after that, it's totally up Dawn," I said, turning to her. She still stood with her head down and looking at the floor. I gently lifted her head with my index finger, making her meet my eyes. "It's all up to you, if you want us to take this child as your own. You have lost so much, and I want you to be able to have the choice. If you choose not to want to take her, I'm sure someone in this room would be more than happy to."

With wide eyes, she shook her head and began to take steps backward. I could see the want in her eyes, but also fear and trepidation. My own look softened. I was still concerned. I wished I could read her mind at that moment. I expected her to flee to the safety of our room, but she went to the window and sat with her knees pulled up to her chest, and wrapped her arms around them. She stared out of the window, lost in thought.

"Has she been this distant all week?" Kaleb asked. I could see Zack and Emily preparing to leave.

"Yeah, she has. Since Erick and Morgan were here. She's been depressed. I've hardly gotten a word out of her, and she hasn't eaten much this week, either," I answered. It was clear she was losing what bit of weight she had been able to gain.

Kaleb had only come by one day, trying to talk to her, but she wouldn't let him anywhere near her. I didn't blame her, although I was extremely worried about her.

"Did one of them say something to scare her?" Kaleb asked, looking over at her.

"I don't think so. I think it's more to do with whatever her panic brought on when she was in that crawl space last week," I answered, watching my girl.

"Hey man, we're gonna head out," Zach said. "You sure you'll be okay with the little one tonight?"

"I'll be fine," I said.

"I'm just a phone call away if you change your mind," he said, before bidding us all goodbye.

"Can I talk to her? I know you aren't your normal self when it comes to her; you're too soft on her," Kaleb said, half amused.

I couldn't deny that I was soft on her. Normally, no one could make me care so deeply about them in such a short amount of time. Most people knew I wasn't one to be messed with.

"Yeah, go ahead," I said with a smile. "I've gotten a lot more out of her today than I have all week."

"Oh, I'll get something out of her," Kaleb said in determination.

"Just be nice," I sighed, worried he'd press the wrong buttons to get her to talk.

"When aren't I?" he winked before going over to my girl. At first, she ignored him, and it took a little coaxing before she slowly followed him out of the room and into a quieter one.

"Maybe she needs anti-depressants," my father said, leaning against the desk beside me.

"I wouldn't want her on those unless there is no other choice," I said, remembering all too well the feeling of everything being muted and dulled.

"It may help her cope with everything," my mom spoke up. "She's been through so much in such a short amount of time."

I probably needed to be a tad bit tougher on her to get through to her; that she couldn't let life get her down, just because her memories got the best of her.

"Not right now," I said, hoping to get my parents to drop the subject.

"Alright, son," my father said, patting my shoulder. "Do you think Dawn will want to keep this child?"

"I honestly have no idea," I sighed, looking down at the baby.

"What do you plan to do if she doesn't?" Mom asked.

"Well, with Emily and Zack expecting a baby within seven months, I don't think they would be up to taking this one on. Emily is strong, but she can only take so much. The both of you aren't up to long nights," I said, looking between my parents. "I think Kelly and Kaleb would be the best option, as they plan to adopt anyways, since they won't be able to have any more biologically."

"If she wants to keep her?" my dad asked.

"Then you'll be grandparents a few months sooner than planned," I laughed lightly. "And I'll have to go shopping."

"What do you hope she decides?" Dad asked.

"My wants are whatever Dawn wants," I answered, looking back down at the baby. She began to stir, looking for food.

"You want her," my mom replied with a smile. I was not going to let my own wants out.

"Mom," I warned, but she merrily chuckled and patted my cheek before going to make a bottle for the baby.

"Do you want us to stay the night? I'm pretty sure the child will be okay, health-wise," my dad said.

"You and Mom can go home. We'll be fine," I yawned.

"You're tired," Mom said, handing me a warm bottle filled with two ounces of formula. "Why haven't you been sleeping?"

"My sleeping partner hasn't slept much. Too many nightmares, but we're just fine," I said, knowing my parents would try to push sleeping pills on her if given the chance.

"Okay, so," Vence said, "We'll head out then. Call if you need anything at all..."

"Of course," I said, taking the bottle away so I could burp the baby.

Mom gave me a hug before leaving, and said they'd call sometime tomorrow so they would know what Dawn and I decided.

CHAPTER 20

DAWN

A tiny whimper woke me up about an hour later. The movie was still playing and the ship had just run into the huge iceberg. I blinked my eyes, trying to figure out what exactly woke me. When the noise happened again, I remembered the baby Elijah had set in the box on the floor.

I slowly made my way out of Elijah's limp hold as he snored on. I looked at him and could see the dark circles around his eyes. I felt bad for keeping him up during the night with the nightmares that plagued me. I didn't want to wake him, so I took a deep breath and moved towards the baby who was searching for food and wiggling around. Her blanket was loose around her.

Slowly and carefully, holding my breath, I picked her up and brought her to my chest while grabbing a diaper from the fabric box.

She was so light compared to Lilly, who was easy to support on her legs and feet now while you held her.

Once in the kitchen and I quickly made her a bottle and

changed her diaper—which was wet—before holding and feeding her. I made my way back to the living room, taking a seat in the oversized chair.

She fit perfectly in my arm.

I knew I was hooked. Her green eyes were open, and she looked up at me as she drank the bottle. She instantly had me captivated. I wasn't sure who her mother was, but I had a feeling Erick was the father, just because he had the reputation of not taking preventative measures.

I made myself comfortable in the chair, holding her to my chest as she went back to sleep. Now I had picked her up, I didn't want to put her down. She was the something worth fighting for. She had me wrapped around her little heart, and I would do just about anything for her.

∼

ELIJAH

I was confused. It was now dark outside, and I was alone on the couch. Glancing at the clock underneath the TV, I read that it was just after midnight, which meant I'd slept on the couch for a solid six hours. I rubbed the sleep from my eyes, feeling more refreshed than I had for weeks.

Sitting up, I looked around the living room, my eyes landing on the oversized chair Dawn was curled up on, sound asleep. Cradled on her chest was the baby, held in both arms and a blanket stuffed up against her so she wouldn't fall. My heart swelled at the sight, and I snapped a picture on my phone of them together.

No wonder I didn't hear the baby. I expected to be woken up shortly after I fell asleep, not knowing if Dawn would get up with her, or if she'd ignore the baby all together. I was happy to see it, knowing there was still life inside her somewhere.

When I'd walked Kaleb out, I asked what they talked about. He wouldn't tell me anything, saying it was all up to her. Whatever it was must have worked, as she ate most of the pizza I sat down in front of her, and now she was taking care of the baby, letting me sleep.

Not wanting to wake either of them up, I gently laid another blanket over them, and took care of the empty bottle lying on the floor.

Not knowing what to do, I sat back down and watched some mindless TV and played on my phone.

I'd only just started to doze back off from boredom when the baby began to stir. I was up and making a bottle by the time Dawn blinked awake. When I came back to give it to her, she was sitting up and changing the baby's diaper again. Dawn's eyes were brighter, and I'm pretty sure a few hours of good sleep had helped her greatly.

"Did you sleep well?" I asked, sitting back down on the couch, facing her.

"Yeah, I did," she said, glancing up at me with a small smile. My own smile broke out at seeing her happy and content—a much better sight than yesterday morning.

"Good to hear," I replied happily. "Is the baby doing okay? No breathing troubles?"

She shook her head, watching the little one eat with a smile.

"Do you want to go back to sleep?" I asked, knowing she had to be tired from lack of sleep, but once again, I only got a no from her as she tended to the baby and got up, moving to sit next to me. "Alright, then how about we play twenty questions? It's where we take turns asking each other things."

"Okay," she said, laying the baby down between us and playing with her hands. I thought the game would be a great way for her to hopefully open up more, since she seemed to be in a better mood for the time being.

"Great, I'll go first," I said. "What's your favorite color?"

"Blue. Yours?" she answered quietly.

"Green," I answered, not even having to think about it. She smiled, knowing my reasoning, and I loved it. "Favorite food?"

"Ice cream, maybe?" she said in thought. "I don't know."

"I'll let you eat whatever you want, whenever you want, until you find your favorite," I promised her. "Mine would be steak."

It went back and forth for about half an hour. I didn't want to ask too many personal questions that would cause her to clam up. There were so many things I wanted to ask to learn more about her, but knew now wasn't the time.

"Can I ask something?" she said quietly.

"Of course," I answered, hiding my surprise.

"Are you going to punish me for the way I acted this past week?" she asked, blushing and looking anywhere but at me. Ah, so she was finally back from wherever her mind had taken her to.

"Do you think you need to be punished?" I asked. I didn't want to, but if it made her feel better, I would.

"I broke your rules. I didn't keep the house in order, and I ignored you," she whispered. "You said I would be punished if I disobeyed."

"Yes, I did," I said, moving to kneel in front of her so she was forced to meet my eyes. I could see the tears gathering. "I also didn't command you in any way to do anything for me. I wanted you to come to me, when you felt better and were able to come to terms with things."

"I didn't do anything for you," she said, her voice breaking.

"I didn't force you to, so you didn't ignore me," I said. "So, do you want to be punished?"

"No," she said instantly, with a quick shake of her head.

"Then I won't. Please, next time you feel so down, come talk to me, alright?"

"Yes, Sir," she answered, relieved, leaning back.

"Anything else?" I asked, seeing her emotions flicker across her face. I could see indecision and worry, but also hope.

"Kaleb said I needed to find something to make me fight," she began quietly. "Something to make me want to fight, to move on, and I think I did."

"What made you decide?" I asked, already having a good idea.

A warm smile spread across her face as her eyes lit up, as she answered. "I lost my own baby, and I wondered what she'd have looked like if she'd lived. I probably wouldn't have been able to keep her or him while I was there, but I still had to wonder. I don't think this one should have to live a life with the fear of feeling alone."

"Kelly and Kaleb would give her everything she needs or wants. Same as I—we—could do," I replied. She picked the baby up as she began to whine.

"I think . . . I want . . ." she mumbled.

"You want to keep her?" I asked, keeping my shock and joy masked as much as I could.

"Please?" she asked, almost begged, as she held the baby to her chest like she was never going to let go.

"Of course," I smiled. "That means we will have to go shopping, or at least I will, to get some things. And we'll need to find a name for her."

"Really?" she asked, sitting up a little too fast and scaring the poor little one. I couldn't help but laugh.

"Yes, really," I clarified with a smile. Her returning smile lit up the room. It was warm and happy, and full of life. "Let me go grab my computer and see what we can find. We may be lucky; the stores may have what we want in stock, furniture wise. I'll send Zack and Emily, and maybe my mother, to pick the items up we need for now. We have to have a car seat for her before she can go out shopping.

"Kaleb heard back with info on the girl, and the timing matches. She'd just been released from social services a month before, so there's no family looking for her," I said, making sure Dawn knew there was no chance that the baby would have to be given up to the next of kin. I'd make sure we were approved to go through the adoption process, even though I saw no reason we wouldn't be able to.

Within the next hour, we had ordered a crib, car seat, stroller, high chair, changing table, and a bunch of clothes. The store was one of the higher priced ones, but would be able to have everything delivered later that day, and installers to set everything up for us. The furniture was all matching cherry wood. We compromised on a simple sleigh style crib, where the bed was close to the floor but easier to lay the baby down.

I knew my parents still had the Moses basket and wicker bassinet they'd used with me and Zack. Kelly would gladly send all the clothes that her little one had outgrown over to us, so for the time being, I believed we were set. I would call Tom and get the paperwork started to make this little one our own. I would be pushing the foster papers through so we didn't have to juggle the baby around from house to house while we waited for approval.

"What will we name her?" I asked, laying the computer on the coffee table, and turning to Dawn.

"Elizabeth?" she asked shyly. It was just a name I've always loved.

"Elizabeth Renea," I replied, giving the baby a middle name after my grandmother, who I'd heard of from stories, as she had passed away when I was too small to remember.

"Perfect," she agreed, stroking the baby's cheek lovingly.

When it was an appropriate time of day, and after feeding and holding Elizabeth—Lizzy—I called Kaleb to ask about the clothes. He wasn't surprised by the outcome, but now joked that I needed to marry my girl. I brushed him off, not wanting to think about that step yet.

I then made a call to Jenks, my lawyer and go-to guy when I needed real documents I couldn't get through legal ways. I got the birth certificate filled out, along with a social security number, and he assured me they'd both be in the mail within weeks. Having ties to the mafia did have its perks.

The last phone call was to my parents, who were both pleasantly surprised and promised to have the over as soon as they got them cleaned up. My mom was happy to be a grandmother.

I held Elizabeth as Dawn went to go take a shower, and I couldn't help but compare how alike they looked. Green eyes, dark hair, and a heart shaped faces. It would be well worth the trouble to make sure this house was baby safe, and every *I* was dotted for the adoption process to be pushed through as quickly as possible.

Emily and Kaleb showed up just as Dawn came down, bringing a brush with her. She silently asked me to do her hair, and I obliged, knowing we both enjoyed it.

"Braid?" I asked as she took a seat on the floor in front of me.

"Sure," she shrugged. "I don't know anything other than a ponytail and braids."

"Yeah, that's about as much as I know too," I softly replied as I began working on her hair. I would need to see about getting her to someone for a trim to even the ends out soon—if she would agree, of course.

Five minutes later, Dawn's soft hair was in a French braid and I went to help Kaleb bring in the boxes and bags of clothes. I knew they had overbought, just because they could. The girls were busy going through one box in the living room, as us guys trekked the others upstairs for later.

"She seems to be in better spirits today," Kaleb

commented as we sat the last of the boxes in the closet so they wouldn't be in the way later. I had chosen the room Dawn would have had as the baby's, and I had Kaleb help me move the bed out and into one of the spare rooms.

"Yes, she is," I agreed, closing the closet door. "Whatever you said to her helped a lot."

"I knew it would," Kaleb said, as we headed back downstairs to our girls.

CHAPTER 21

DAWN

I finally felt like I belonged. I couldn't help but watch Elijah with Lizzy. He was a natural, and it made me love him even more. I did have to wonder where his Dom side was hiding, since I'd hardly seen it. I asked about it as we looked through the most adorable cute girl clothes, hoping to find something that would fit our baby.

Lilly was on her tummy, chewing on her hands and watching what was going on around her. Lizzy lay wiggling on a blanket not too far from me. I could see them both being the best of friends as they grew up, and it helped to make me feel like I'd made the right choice.

"He's always been soft around you," Emily had said "I bet when the time comes to the bedroom activities, it will show up. He seems to be tamer in that aspect since you came back into his life."

I blushed bright red as the idea gave me warm butterflies in my belly, and Emily laughed at me. I couldn't wipe the smile off my face.

"Do you think he really likes me that way? I know I haven't been the best since I've been here and all . . ." I trailed off.

"Of course he does! You haven't been ready for that, but you will be soon. You're asking about it, so don't deny that you like the idea."

I smiled shyly as I heard the boys come back down the stairs. I had to admit to myself, I was curious. It was a fascinating lifestyle, and I think I was getting to the point that I wanted to know more, to have that type of relationship—as long as it stayed in the bedroom.

"When will the furniture be here?" Emily asked, looking up from the pile of clothes she had laid out across her lap.

"Around noon," Elijah answered through a yawn.

"Long night?" Kaleb asked, taking a seat on the sofa.

"Not really. Dawn took care of Lizzy, so I got a good night's sleep," Elijah said, winking at me. I blushed and looked down. Emily laughed lightly as Kaleb snorted in reply.

"Lizzy?" Kaleb asked with a raised brow.

"Elizabeth Renea," I whispered, looking over at her. Lizzy had fallen asleep on the floor, while Lilly continued to play.

"Pretty name," Emily said. "How about we go put some of these clothes away while the boys keep an eye on the babies."

For the next hour, Emily and I worked together putting the clothes in the dresser and closet.

"Maybe next week, if you're up to it, we can go shopping for some baby stuff that you may need by then. Like toys and such," Emily said, flattening the box out so it could be stored easily.

"I think Elijah ordered everything we possibly could need," I said, taking a seat on the floor. "Other than diapers and formula, at least."

"Well, we still should go shopping sometime soon, as long as it's safe for you to," Emily said. "We can take the boys if need be. No one will even think about trying anything with both of them close."

After we went back downstairs, Joslyn and Vence showed up, bringing a good number of items along with them.

They both took turns holding Lizzy, and even feeding her. Vence checked her over again, saying he wouldn't predict any health issues with her size that would cause any trouble. We just needed to get her into his office in about a week or so to start her immunizations, and to discuss which ones would be best to give her.

Joslyn had brought a pan of pre-made enchiladas, which Elijah put in the oven to melt the cheese and warm it up.

"I let your brother know this morning when he called," Joslyn said, turning to Elijah who was laid out on the floor, next to Lilly. She had taken a cat nap and was now talking in her own way to him.

"I figured you would," Elijah replied.

"How long will you be home, anyway, son?" Vence asked as he brought drinks in for all of us.

"However long I want to be. I may go back after the trials start, part time. I don't think I'll be going back full time, but I also can't just stay home all the time, either," Elijah replied, getting up from the floor. He came around and sat beside me on the loveseat, wrapping an arm around my shoulders.

"When will the trials start? Do you know?" Joslyn asked.

"Not sure yet, but hopefully we'll know a date soon. The lawyers are getting their evidence organized and all that," Kaleb said as his phone began to ring. He sighed before excusing himself and mumbling something about taking time off from everything too, when things got quiet again.

"That should be the delivery people," Elijah said as the intercom buzzed. He went to the front door to let them in through the gate. He had switched the code used to get in, with only his family having it, since Morgan was able to somehow get past the gate.

"I do hope you didn't let him order the most expensive things in the store. Babies don't care what they have as long as they have love and food," Joslyn laughed.

"He tried to," I replied shyly, remembering how we had trouble agreeing on what to purchase.

"Lizzy and you will have everything both of you could dream of. If you have more kids later, they will be spoiled rotten," Joslyn laughed. "By everyone."

"Of course, they will," Kelly agreed, taking the conversation off me.

"How?" Kaleb growled from the kitchen before hushing his voice again. After a few minutes, while Elijah was telling the delivery people where to put everything, Kaleb came back in, looking upset and not pleased at all.

"I'll go get the food out of the oven," Emily said, giving Kaleb a look that meant he was to follow her. I didn't think I would ever be able to pull a look like that off.

"And the highchair will go in the kitchen," Elijah said as the green and blue highchair was brought into the house.

"You got it," the man spoke in a raspy voice.

"The crib is set up where you wanted it, Mr. Brown," the man said as he came back downstairs. "Is there anything else you need?"

"That will be all. Thank you, gentlemen," Elijah said as he stood up from the couch where he was sitting beside me.

They left shortly after, saying to contact the store if something didn't seem to be set up correctly. Joslyn brought us girls out a plate of food, laughing at the looks on the guys' faces when they were told to go get their own.

Elijah's parents didn't stay around much longer, since Joslyn and Emily had made plans to go shopping that afternoon for a few baby items we apparently couldn't live without. I wasn't sure what they could possibly be, as it seemed like we had everything we could need for the first year of Lizzy's life.

"Seth called," Kaleb said, looking at Elijah. "Morgan and Joan posted bail."

"How?" Elijah asked, glaring at Kaleb. Although, I wasn't all that surprised.

"No idea. That's what I wanted to know. The person who gave the money over wasn't caught on tape, and no name was given."

"The bail was high enough that no one should have been able to pay it."

"That's what I thought, too. Morgan must have ties to people we didn't know about. Galvin hasn't even tried to bail like I expected," Kaleb said.

"I wonder what Morgan is hiding, then, since I'm sure he ran off to one of his hideouts."

"He'll come out soon enough," Kaleb said. "I do need to run to the office for a few hours to look at the tape myself, and a few other things. So, we'll leave you three be."

"I'll see you soon," Emily said, giving me a hug goodbye.

The house seemed quiet, and after turning the TV on, we both took an hour's nap until Lizzy demanded to be fed.

CHAPTER 22

ELIJAH

The next couple of weeks went by smoothly, considering everything that had been going on before then. Dawn had no nightmares, and she seemed to be doing much better. She still had quiet moments, but she had always been the quiet type of person, even when she was younger. Lizzy was a month old, and the papers I needed had come in. Dawn and I were officially Elizabeth's parents. The DNA test results came back, so Kaleb and I knew that the girl, Joanna Miller, was the mother. She was in social services for years, and she ended up aging out of the system. The DNA also matched Erick, so there was no question about who Jessica was spending her time with before she was eighteen.

Joanna's body was thoroughly autopsied, and the doctor found out that the baby was at least eight months in the womb, just from looking at the placenta. I was happy to find out that Elizabeth wasn't as young as we first thought—she was just small, but that could easily be because her mother didn't eat well, or took drugs.

We hadn't ventured out much because I had a feeling Morgan had something planned, and I didn't want him to have any chance of getting to Dawn. In the interview Kaleb had conducted with both him and Joan, they had hinted that they would do anything to have her back. Why, we had no idea.

Morgan had said he'd be back to get what was his. I was more than willing to move, but Dawn wouldn't let me do that.

"I like it here. I can't see me being comfortable anywhere else I know you haven't been," Dawn had said. I didn't make us pack everything and move within days, like I wanted. I did purchase an apartment that was furnished with everything we needed, in case we had to leave at a moment's notice.

Kelly and Kaleb had been over a few times, and we'd played a couple of card games, just having fun. Somehow, Kaleb talked us into playing a truth game. I groaned, not knowing how Dawn would take to all this, but at least us guys were still coherent and hardly had much to drink at all; someone would have to get up with the babies.

"I'll go first . . . Elijah, what is your favorite position?" Kaleb started.

"Do you really want to know?" I asked, raising an eyebrow.

"Yup," he nodded.

"I'd have to say…doggy style, or spread eagle…can't decide between them."

"I love doggy," Kelly said brightly with a giggle.

Dawn sat there staring at me, with only a slight blush. I couldn't help but wink at her, making her blush darker.

"I like any style," Kaleb said with a shrug. "I'm not picky. I do love to be on the bottom sometimes, when the opportunity arises."

"Dawn?" Kelly asked with a smile, waiting for her to answer. I really didn't expect her to.

"Um, I don't know," Dawn answered, looking off to the side.

"That's okay. Eli will help you figure that out," Kelly laughed.

"Okay . . . Elijah, your turn," Kaleb said.

"Alright. What's your favorite TV show?" I asked.

"Ohh! Anything with vampires. They are sooo hot," Kelly said dreamily. "Vampire guys are yummy to look at."

"I'm more into anything supernatural," Kaleb said. "Two guys fighting demons…now *that* is entertaining."

"Oh, that angel guy is cute," Kelly winked.

"Where was your first kiss?" Dawn asked bashfully.

"Which first kiss? I've had a few," Kaleb winked.

"Any first kiss, I guess," she shrugged.

"Hmm. Well, with Elijah, my first kiss was in my playroom. With Kelly, it was at the club where we met," Kaleb answered easily.

"Hmm. That was a great first kiss," Kelly said, licking her lips after taking another drink.

"What about you, Dawn?" I asked, not letting my eyes fall from hers as she sat next to me.

"I've never really been kissed—not that I've been able to like, at least," she said sadly. I had briefly kissed her weeks ago, but it was just a peck, so it didn't count as a first kiss. At least not to me.

"Well, can we change that," I said, leaning my forehead against hers.

She nodded, before taking the few inches that separated our lips. Her lips were soft and warm as they met mine. I wasn't going to push it any further, but I let my lips stay there until she pulled away. Her cheeks were red, but her eyes were lit with happiness.

I couldn't help but press my lips to hers again a few more times because Kaleb whistled at us, making her blush more.

Most of the night went like that, each of us asking questions everyone had to answer to some extent. Dawn didn't really ask anything personal, but she answered a few here and there that she could. She hadn't watched much TV or movies, so she didn't know what to answer.

By the time midnight rolled around, both girls were nearly passed out and there were two hungry babies. I sent them up to bed while Kaleb and I took care of kids. Lizzy was still small to be a month and a half old but was healthy. At least there were no delays in her growth, except she didn't eat as much in one setting, and sometimes was hungry an hour afterward, while other times she could wait up to four hours to eat.

Once Lizzy and Lilly were both fed and changed, we made our way upstairs to put them in their beds. We had recently bought a playpen we'd set up in the spare room. We couldn't help but laugh when we saw both girls passed out on the same bed. Of course we took pictures, because drunk nights were always something that had to be documented.

Turning the light off after I grabbed the bassinet and I wheeled it into the spare room, we decided we'd just sleep together, as we'd done it before with no issues. Plus, we'd be woken up by the little ones soon enough.

"Think the girls would be mad if we woke them up early in the mornin'?" Kaleb asked as he laid on the bed.

"Kelly would," I laughed quietly so I didn't wake the sleeping babies.

"You're right. She'd have my balls, and more," Kaleb yawned. "Now, no cuddlin'."

"You're the one who likes to steal the covers," I joked, remembering how we would always fight over them.

"Whatever," he mumbled sleepily.

DAWN

That next morning, I woke up with the sun shining brightly through the crack in the curtains. It seemed to be brighter than normal, so I squinted against it as I slowly made my way out of bed, leaving it empty. I padded towards the bathroom, hoping a shower would help clear the fog that covered my sleepy brain.

My lips tingled, thinking about that kiss. I hadn't willingly kissed anyone before. Elijah's lips were soft and warm. I didn't expect them to be so . . . perfect. I was used to hard, demanding lips tainted by drugs or cigarettes.

It was so much better than the little peck weeks ago, before Morgan showed up, and before I had to come to the conclusion that I had a reason to live, to get better, and try to be someone Elijah and Lizzy could possibly deserve.

I was falling for Elijah—hard. I'm not sure when it happened, but my heart beat for him. It could have been watching him with Lizzy, being there for me when I needed him the most, or everything all together.

Last night was fun, and I learned a few things I didn't know about everyone, myself included.

When I got downstairs, things didn't seem so bright. The smell of pancakes and bacon was in the air, making my stomach growl. I had started eating more, which made Elijah more than happy. Reaching the kitchen, I saw Kelly sitting with her head in her hands, while Kaleb laughed at her.

"Good mornin'," Elijah said, giving me a hug once I reached him at the counter, where he was finishing off the last batch of pancakes. "Sleep good?"

"Hmmhm," I answered, not wanting to part from him. I craved his warmth and never wanted to leave if I didn't have to.

"Good," Elijah said with a smile. "How 'bout you go sit down? I'll bring the food over." I was hoping he'd kiss me again, afraid to take charge and do it myself.

Knowing he wouldn't let me help, I took a seat at the table. Lilly was in the high chair, looking around, while Lizzy was in the swing, fast asleep. She had grown and was an absolute joy. Joslyn loved to spoil her, and she had so many things already, I didn't think she'd ever want for anything.

Last week, Elijah had taken me to a clothing store to pick out some I could choose myself. I didn't really want much, nor need anything, but to make him happy, I picked out a few nicer things. I was starting to find my clothing tighter as I gained weight.

Last time I looked in the mirror, I could see my green eyes were brighter, and my face wasn't as thin. My ribs were no longer black and blue. It took them the longest to heal. I was happy I was looking better, knowing that it pleased Elijah.

"Since you're both finally up among the living," Kaleb began as we all started to eat, "the trial start date, for at least Galvin and a few others, will start January 27th. As of right now, they have enough evidence against them that Dawn won't need to testify. Her statement, along with her signed affidavit, is more than enough. Plus, a few of his guys gave out more information, thinking they could get less time."

"I thought mafia families were tight and didn't rat anyone of their own out," Kelly said between bites.

"Yes, they usually don't. It's clear as day that this mafia team is not as tight as the bigger ones. Galvin won't be seeing the light of day for a very long time," Kaleb went on. "Most of his men will be in the same position."

"What about Morgan?" I asked. He had yet to be found—same with my mother. I wasn't even sure I wanted to call her my mother anymore.

"Once he is found, and there is a nationwide search for him and Joan, he will be put in jail without bail. Now, since he is a flight risk, and the one who captured the most girls off the streets, his will be a more detailed trial. They may want you to testify against him and your mother, since you once did live with him. But you don't have to if you really don't want to," Kaleb answered.

"What will happen if I don't?" I asked, needing to know so I could think about what I should do.

"Once again, with the evidence we have against him, he would be sentenced to life. If he has a lawyer half as good as Elijah's, he may be able to get less and be out within twenty years. Same with Joan. If they have any type of money to have that type of lawyer, that means if you testify, you could be rewarded money for the abuse you were subjected to."

"I don't want money, I want them to pay for what they did," I said.

"Of course, you don't," Elijah said with a smile. "You've hardly wanted anything at all."

"Why would I? I don't need anything more than I have now," I simply answered.

Elijah gave me a look that said more than words ever could. It was filled with happiness and hope, and something else I couldn't place.

CHAPTER 23

DAWN

*B*efore I knew it, it was a week before Christmas. The house was decorated with lights, and we had a big fake tree in front of the windows in the living room. A few presents, mostly from Elijah, were already under it. I had yet to figure out what to get him since he'd never once said what he wanted. I had ordered Lizzy a few things that were already wrapped and under the tree. She was now four months old and was just starting to really play with toys. Between Joslyn and Emily, she had nearly everything she already could ever want.

There was at least a foot of snow on the ground, and I'd been able to take a walk in it while Joslyn watched Lizzy a couple of times. I wasn't too fond of the snow but enjoyed how the sun would sparkle off it. I wasn't much into the cold, either—not since I'd been kept in it for years.

Joslyn had brought over a couple boxes of fleece material, thinking maybe I could come up with a craft idea for when Lizzy took her naps. Most of the time so far, I just wrote in my journal. It had helped me immensely. I wrote down everything I could remember, from living with both loving parents, to my time in the prison. Even now, I wondered if Joan had ever loved me.

Elijah and I had been able to go out and do a little shopping here and there, but we never stayed out too long. He was worried about Morgan trying to get to us. It was only a matter of time before he would pop up, and Kaleb was sure that it would be when we least expected it.

Weeks ago, I was happy to hear that my blood tests came back clean. My iron levels were leveling out, and I wasn't as tired as I used to be. The diet, which consisted of eating just about anything I could possibly want, had helped greatly.

We had yet been able to enjoy the pool and hot tub, even when Kaleb and Kelly were here, since we didn't want to leave two babies wondering around. Lilly was now starting to crawl. We would have to plan time soon for Joslyn or Emily to watch Lizzy while we spent a little time in the pool without having to worry about her.

Elijah was currently giving Lizzy a bath, while I was enjoying some quiet time in front of the fireplace, watching the snow fall. Everything had been quiet recently in the news about Galvin and his henchmen being brought down.

Elijah had been keeping a close eye on it, wanting to know what people thought about the whole thing. My name was not released to keep my identity hidden. Elijah's was never mentioned or posted online. I was surprised it was so quiet after all that went down.

Nothing we already didn't know ever came out, and most of what did was just speculation. The media thought Galvin was the one to turn himself in, and he'd brought all his followers down with him.

"Hey," Elijah said, coming to stand beside me, holding a freshly clean baby who was all smiles. We'd just started giving her oatmeal twice a day, and it ended up in her dark hair more often than not.

"Hi," I said, looking at him with a smile.

"How about we watch some good old Christmas movies? I don't plan to go anywhere in this weather. We're under a blizzard watch." I looked out the window and noticed the sun was covered with dark clouds, creating a dark, dreary day.

After putting Lizzy in the swing, the only way she would sleep during the day, Elijah put on *Home Alone*. With a blanket covering us, he pulled me between his legs with my back against his front.

I leaned against him as he began to kiss the side of my neck, unable to help but lean to one side, allowing him more access.

"You smell wonderful," Elijah said, placing kisses along my throat and up my jawline. His hands slowly moved to my waist and up to the underside of my breasts. I arched into him, wanting more. I didn't have a bra on, so he had easy access.

"More?" I asked, panting. The fire below burned, needing a release.

He didn't hesitate to move his hand up higher, over the hardened peak of my nipples. I could feel his calloused hands rubbing with just the right pressure—not too soft, but not hard, either.

"We may have fifteen minutes," Elijah said huskily. "Lizzy won't stay asleep much longer."

"Please, Sir," I said, knowing that would be more than enough time to at least get a little pleasure. *I'll let him have an early Christmas gift tonight, then,* I thought as I blushed.

"Are you sure?" Elijah asked, kissing the side of my neck again and sucking. I was sure he'd leave a mark, and I didn't mind one bit.

"Yes," I moaned, drawing the word out.

"You'll have to stay quiet," he warned, moving one hand down slowly to the waist of my yoga pants.

"I can be quiet, Sir," I said, almost pleading for him to touch me again where I needed him the most at that moment.

"We'll see about that," he laughed lightly before gently nibbling my earlobe. I took a deep breath at the sensation, not knowing if I wanted more of it or less.

One hand stayed at my breasts, playing and rolling my nipples, making me moan quietly, while the other hand made its way past my underwear. His fingers were warm and began to touch and play with my lower lips lightly, making me crave more—so much more.

"You shaved," he breathed out.

"Yeah. Emily said guys . . . liked it better," I said, trying to not push against his hand to make it go where I wanted.

"I do like it, more than you could ever know," he whispered with a lust filled voice, rubbing my clit and inserting a finger into me.

"Ooh," I moaned, closing my eyes and feeling how strong he was. It had been at least two months since I'd had any kind of release, and so much had happened between then and now. I could feel his heat soak into me.

"You're so wet," he moaned, adding another finger. I could feel him hard behind me and would have gladly taken him in my hand if I could have reached comfortably. "Are you wet for me?"

"Always," I breathed out as he hit the spot that brought me so much pleasure.

He knew exactly what I needed. He rubbed his palm against my clit as he began a faster rhythm, pumping his fingers in and out of my body. He pinched my nipple harder, and I came instantly. He continued, slowly pumping in and out until my climax subsided.

With a smile, Elijah removed his fingers from me. "Better?"

"Much. Thank you," I said, keeping my eyes closed and basking in the after effects. I never wanted to move.

A few minutes later, Lizzy had other ideas, crying out loudly for attention. With me groaning and Elijah laughing, I moved to pick up my daughter with a smile while Elijah went to wash his hands and make a bottle. I changed her diaper and enjoyed the time I had with her.

I wished the path I had to take to get here hadn't happened the way it did; I would have loved to skip most of the things that had happened to me, but I couldn't change it. If I hadn't been sold by my mother, I wouldn't have found this baby, and maybe not Elijah. Just because we grew up together, doesn't mean we would have stayed close.

I was beginning to have the craving for my own children with Elijah—at least one, maybe two, but I wasn't sure if I was up to going through the checkups to see if I could still have children. I knew from what Emily had said just the week before that the depo shot stayed in a woman's system for quite some time after the last dose, and I didn't know what kind of damage had been done when Erick had forced me to lose the baby I had carried.

I had yet to get my period, but I wasn't concerned. Vence had said it may take some time, taking in my weight loss and stress. If I didn't have it by the time I fully decided to have children of my own, I would bring it up to someone.

For the time being, I was more than happy with how life was turning out. I was happy, content, and falling more in love with Elijah and our daughter.

CHAPTER 24

ELIJAH

The snow was piled high by the time Christmas morning arrived. I snuck downstairs early to set the rest of Dawn's gifts under the brightly lit tree. We had decorated it the week after Thanksgiving. The white tree nearly touched the high vaulted ceilings. Lizzy loved looking at the multicolored lights; they kept her entertained for a few minutes at a time, sometimes up to an hour.

There was already a number of gifts under the tree for all three of us, and a few for the rest of the family and our close friends. Kelly, Kaleb and Lily would be over tomorrow to celebrate with us. Once Dawn was up, along with Lizzy, we would open our own gifts here at the house, spending our first holiday together as a family.

Deciding it was late enough, I began to make us breakfast: blueberry pancakes, bacon, and eggs. I had the radio on low, listening to the music while I cooked.

Flipping the last few pancakes over, I sang along to a song, moving my body with the rhythm.

I instantly knew when Dawn entered the kitchen. I could feel my skin tingle before she ever came up behind me, wrapping her arms around my waist and laying her face against my back. Her body was warm, and mine responded.

Looking into her eyes, I could see so much happiness there, finally. It had taken long enough.

"Thank you, again, for last night," I said before I kissed her warm lips. She replied, pushing into me and grabbing my shirt tightly, trying to pull me closer to her.

We had just gone to bed, making sure Lizzy was sound asleep. We left the door ajar, since she was now across the hall in her own bed, even though we had a baby monitor. I normally slept naked, but sharing the bed with someone who had been abused, I decided it would be best to not go completely bare. It wasn't until just a few weeks ago that I started to sleep in my boxers and not in pj bottoms.

I was lying on the bed under the covers, propped up against the pillows and waiting for Dawn. She was taking longer than normal in the bathroom. I was just about to get up and go check on her when she came out, looking like sin.

She wore her long dark hair down but pinned back off her face as she slowly made her way out of the bathroom. Her eyes were downcast, looking up at me through her eyelashes. She wore a skimpy black baby doll nighty that pushed her breasts up, making them seem bigger than they normally were. I briefly wondered where she got it. Then my brain froze when it dawned on me what she wanted.

With flushed cheeks, both from arousal and embarrassment, she moved her hands down her own body, starting at her sides, down her hips, and along her creamy thighs.

I was lost for words as I gawked at her. My mouth was wide open, along with my eyes. I couldn't take them off her, not for a second. Nor could I form any coherent thoughts.

"Do I look okay?" Dawn asked all too sweetly as she tilted her head to the side. Oh, the little minx knew exactly what she was doing to me.

"Uh . . . yeah," I managed to get out in a daze. Blinking, I swallowed. Loudly.

"Are you okay?" she asked with a smirk.

"More than."

She slowly made her way to the bed, walking at a slow pace, allowing me to watch her. She deliberately crawled over me, one knee on each side of my legs, her arms supporting her as she leaned down and met my lips. She was gentle, pressing once, twice, a third time before lifting back a few inches. The look she gave me was filled with want.

"Are you sure?" I half moaned, letting my hands finally grip her around her waist. I only had to press my hard cock up a few short inches and I would have been meeting her warmth.

"Very," she moaned, leaning down to give me another searing kiss, this time tempting me by licking my lips. Her hardened nipples brushed against my torso.

"Tell me to stop and I will," I said, giving her another chance to back down.

"I need you," she said breathlessly, pushing her warm center against me.

Not able to fight the urge any longer, I moved my hand down to her ass, finding her sans underwear. I was a hot mess, knowing she'd planned this without giving away her nerves the entire day.

"Dawn," I said before I traced my lips down her neck, sucking and marking her as mine. I loved seeing my marks on her. "If you play with fire, you may get burned."

"Maybe I want to be burned," she moaned, pressing down on my throbbing erection.

Deciding to not test my limits—or hers—I helped her lift her nighty over her head. Her breasts bounced as her hair fell over them, teasing me with the view.

She lifted her body so I could strip my boxers off in one swift move. Dawn set back down, her pussy right over my stiffness, rubbing her clit against me. I moved my hand to her wet pussy, *stroking her, feeling the wetness that seeped out, coating my fingers easily.*

I took my fingers, one and then the other, and placed them in my mouth while she watched, sucking her sweetness off them. She moaned, grinding her pussy to my cock, and she was bringing me closer to the edge but I held fast, staving off my orgasm, knowing I could easily have one like this. I wanted to come inside her.

Dawn, who must have been reading my mind, lifted herself, took hold of my cock and slowly pushed down on me. I slid into her, inch by slow inch. I could feel her tight walls around me, squeezing me tightly. I nearly came on the spot.

"I'm not gonna last," I managed to groan out breathily.

"Neither am I," she panted out, pausing once I was sheathed inside her.

She was extremely tight and warm as her pussy sucked me in. She slowly began to move, making her breasts jiggle. I couldn't help but raise up and take one of her breasts in my mouth. I sucked and nibbled, making her to moan, and she began to speed up her thrusts.

With one hand, I grabbed her waist, pulling her breast further into my mouth. I took my fingers and ran them down her body, rubbing where we were joined together, getting my fingers wet with her juices. I took one slick with her wetness and circled her hole. She clenched around me and cried out in pleasure, her walls sucking me so hard I came immediately, unable to hold out any longer. I don't think there was a drop of cum left in my balls at that point.

Dawn fell on top of my body, both of us panting; we just lay there, gently kissing and staying relaxed in each other's arms, neither one of us wanting to move.

"Merry Christmas," I whispered.

"I'm glad you liked it," she said, turning red as she tried to hide her face against my chest.

"I more than liked it," I said, kissing the top of her head. "Now go sit. I'm sure that little girl won't like to be waiting any more for her own food."

I fed Lizzy in between bites while Dawn enjoyed her

warm food. She took care of the dishes while I cleaned our daughter up before we made our way to the living room. We worked perfectly together.

Once Dawn sat on the couch holding Lizzy, I handed out the few presents I'd bought them both, putting my own presents on the table. I wanted to watch my girls open their gifts first.

Dawn helped Lizzy open her three gifts. One was a blanket she'd made from the material my mom had dropped off a few weeks ago. There was also a toy Lizzy had yet to get from the grandparents. She was little enough that she really didn't care. The other was a stuffed animal from me.

"Open yours," I said, nodding to her own pile.

She slowly picked up the first one. I knew she had never truly had many gifts for any holiday even before she was taken, so I could have bought her so many if I'd wanted to. She deserved everything she could ever want, but I also knew she didn't want much, and I didn't even know *what* she wanted. I just hoped she'd like what I'd ordered for her.

∽

DAWN

Slowly opening the first gift, I couldn't help the smile that spread across my face. It was a simple necklace with a charm of a mother and daughter.

The next gift was a few books I'd mentioned wanting to read, as I'd read all the books Elijah had ordered for me before. These books were young adult ones but contained more of a mystery theme to them.

In one slim box was the adoption papers to make Elizabeth our baby—our very own.

The last gift was lightweight and in a square box. Glancing up at Elijah, I slowly opened it.

Inside was an iPad, already turned on and loaded full of apps. I had started to play around with Elijah's—with his help, of course—just two weeks before. This one already had a protective drop case around it.

"Thank you," I said, happy and content with what he had gotten me. I was worried he would want to go overboard.

"Not a problem," he smiled.

After I nodded my head, motioning towards his own gifts, he opened the top one. I had Emily pick up a few things for me, not knowing what to get him for sure. Emily had decided to get him an iTunes gift card, and a few new history books.

The last gift was stuffed into a box I was able to find in the attic just the day before while Emily kept Elijah busy over something in the kitchen so I could finish wrapping it.

He pulled out a fleece tie blanket, which would be more than big enough for both of us to cuddle up on the couch. It was blue camo on one side, while the other side was gray. I'd been working on it off and on all week while Emily had been over, declaring that we needed girl time.

She was the one who had helped me come up with the idea off Pinterest. I had been addicted to that site since she'd introduced me to it. I found a lot of crafts and recipes I couldn't wait to try.

"You made this?" Elijah asked in awe. He knew I'd made Lizzy one, but not him.

"Yes," I answered, not sure if he really liked it or not.

"It's wonderful. Thank you!" he said, giving me a huge hug. "Emily helped?"

"Just to keep you preoccupied all week," I said shyly.

"Thank you," he repeated.

We shared a few more kisses and some innocent touching before getting ready to go to Joslyn and Vence's house for lunch.

∼

Arriving at the Hunter family home, the sun was finally beginning to shine through the clouds. The roads had been cleared of snow long before we ever left the warmth of the house. Lizzy was covered by her new blanket as I carried her to the warming car. I wore a new coat Kelly had ordered for me shortly after I got here, knowing I would need it sooner or later. Underneath, I had on a pair of skinny jeans—the most comfortable things next to yoga pants—and a long sweater that was not too tight but showed off my weight gain.

Kelly had been right, I did have to get more clothes as I gained weight, and it would be another year before I knew for sure if I was done gaining back the weight that I had lost. I didn't need too many, but nicer ones as Elijah had been taking me out of the house at least a couple times a month now.

"Hello, dears," Joslyn said with a hug before she stole my girl from my hands, and proceeded to get her out of the contraption called a car seat. I could hear Lizzy coo at her loving grandmother.

"Sure, just ignore us. I'll make my way to the food myself," Elijah said, pouting and making fun of his mother.

"Oh, hush you," Joslyn said, waving Elijah off with a laugh.

"Elijah, Dawn," Vence greeted us, smiling at his wife. "Hope the roads were clear for you."

"Yeah, they were just fine," Elijah said as they patted each other on the back.

"Good, good," he replied. "Everyone is in the living room already."

"The food is almost done," Joslyn said as she led the way to the living room after setting the seat next to the door so it'd be out of the way.

Emily beamed when she saw us enter. Zack sat watching the TV and hooting about something. Elijah sat by him as Emily moved to me. I knew the two were looking into adoption and had a child they would be meeting in a few weeks to see if they were a good match.

"So, did he like it?" she asked, hinting towards the blanket.

"Yes, he loved it," I answered brightly.

"I told you he would," she laughed, giving me a small hug. We had gotten closer, almost as close as sisters, in the short time we'd been together.

Looking over towards the corner, I saw their own Christmas tree, but with more presents.

"They always go overboard," Emily said with a laugh. "At least, that's what Zack says. I wouldn't know."

I had almost forgotten that Emily and I both had been prisoners of hell at one time. It seemed so long ago with everything that had happened since then. I was different, finally starting to figure out who I was and what I wanted out of life.

"Well, they have one grandchild, plus another on the way, to spoil rotten," I laughed.

"Yeah, true," Emily said with a bright smile.

"Oh, Dawn, dear, can I have your help in the kitchen for a moment?" Joslyn asked.

Giving Emily a look asking her what was up, she merrily smiled and shook her head, not letting me in on the big secret. Sighing, I made my way to the kitchen, following Joslyn.

"How are you doing?" Joslyn asked as she busied herself stirring the mashed potatoes in a black pot on the stove.

"Good," I answered, not sure what she was trying to do. I watched her, hoping she'd give something away.

"You and Elijah seem to be getting close," she observed. Well, of course, we were. We did live together. And the man had saved me in a way I never thought would be possible. "Have you thought about the future at all?" she asked, turning to face me.

"Some," I shrugged. "I thought about maybe getting my GED, at least."

I had wanted to at least have my GED to feel more normal but now with the choice of what I wanted to do, I could do anything—almost. The best place to start was to finish my education. I couldn't see myself doing college, but I wanted my daughter to grow up with parents who had, at least, both finished high school.

"Well, that's good. The nearby college offers online classes. I'm sure Elijah would be willing to help you set it up," Joslyn said, bringing the rolls out of the oven. "How do you feel about Elijah?"

"What?" I asked, shocked that she'd ask that.

"What do you feel for Elijah?" she repeated with a smile.

"Um, I don't know…"

"Do you love him?" she asked, looking at me in a motherly way.

"Yes," I whispered quietly, looking down. I was in love with him, and I couldn't see how my life would be without him there.

"He loves you just as much, you know," Joslyn said, bending so she could meet my eyes. "He has always loved you, and will love you till the end of his days."

I couldn't help but smile, looking up to the only real mother figure I'd ever had. I could see Elijah loved me, even after everything I had been through. He was there, helping to hold me while I fell apart at the seams and after he saved me, bringing life back into me. If it wasn't for him, I wouldn't be here today.

"Now, I wanted to give you this without everyone watching," Joslyn said, handing me a scrapbook. The book was covered in blue and white flowers, with '*Memories*' written in the middle in cursive writing.

I slowly opened it, seeing pictures of my parents and pictures of me with Elijah and Zack as we all grew up. There were some current pictures of all of us, showing me just how much I had changed in the last three months.

"Thank you," I said with tears in my eyes. I understood why she did this without everyone else watching, and it made me feel loved—like I belonged here.

"You're very welcome, dear child," she said, giving me a hug. "You have always been like a daughter to me, no matter what has happened."

Shortly after I got my tears under control, she called everyone in for lunch. We all sat at the big round table as we ate and joked around. I listened to the boys tease each other, laughing at the childhood stories they shared.

After we finished eating, we all went back to the living room to open presents. Lizzy got new clothes and even more toys, which she really didn't need. I smiled, rolling my eyes at just how extravagant our family was. I guess when having as much money as this family did, it didn't really matter.

It was dark out by the time we left, the trunk of the car packed full of everything we had been given that day. I was surprised the time went by so fast, and that I had enjoyed it. I was able to get to know my new family better, without any worry that any of them would ever turn their back and hurt me like my mother had.

CHAPTER 25

ELIJAH

On the way home, I paid close attention to the side streets, knowing that Morgan was out there, watching. I made sure I kept my cool to not let Dawn know. I was afraid she would panic after such a great day.

It was the best day I could ask for.

My dad and brother, of course, had to bombard me with questions as they could see Dawn and I were getting closer. Dad wanted to know my plans for the future, and I gladly told him that I wanted to make Dawn my wife but knew it wasn't the right time yet.

We had everything put away and Lizzy in bed shortly before the news came on. I had taken to watching it nightly, sometimes even in the mornings, to keep up to date with what they'd found out about the brothel that was taken down. I had to make sure our names were kept out, since I didn't want to be tied to it in any way—at least, not yet. There were still a few men around who needed to be caught.

Dawn and I were on the couch covered by the soft blanket

she'd made me. The baby monitor was set up on the side table so we could hear Lizzy if she woke up.

"New tonight is the upcoming trial of Galvin Holt, the leader of the brothel recently taken down in Seattle. He was taken into custody November 1st at a client's home where he was trying to sell a girl for her services. We have yet to get a name of the client, who is under FBI protection to bring this mafia family down. The girl in question has not been identified, although a number of other women have stepped forward against Galvin and his workings," the newscaster said. The TV was filled with random pictures of Galvin, a few of his men, and a few other women who had been sold. I hadn't seen any of the women, but they were all placed around the states in protective services.

"The Bench Trial is set to start January 5th, at nine a.m. We have not been able to talk to Galvin himself, as he is requesting that no one comes to interview him until his lawyer is able to be present," he concluded before they went to another story about the current train derailment in Colorado that was spilling oil into the Platt river.

The same story was on the rest of the week, with no new information. I wasn't taking chances and kept Dawn and Lizzy home most of the time. Dawn didn't ask why, so I didn't say anything, although she was smart, so she probably knew my reasoning without me having to say anything.

Kaleb and I were some of the last to arrive at the courthouse a month later. A few news crews were poised and ready to shoot pictures of anything and everything they possibly could about the case.

We stayed quiet as we entered the courtroom, filled with a number of people. No one spared us a glance as we took our seats up near the front of the room. The people were talking among themselves, too quiet for me to really hear anything. I wore a beanie over my hair so I wasn't too recognizable. I also hadn't shaved for a few days.

"Any luck on getting the judge to talk to you?" I asked. Kaleb had wanted an idea on what to expect during this trial, since Morgan had many charges against him and was still missing.

"No. I don't think he even knows yet for sure," Kaleb replied as the guards came in, telling everyone to rise as the judge entered.

"You may take your seats," Judge Garrett Johnsville spoke as he took his own at the high podium. His sandy hair was pulled back so it wasn't in his face as he took his time looking over the papers lying on his desk.

In the front row of the pews sat Galvin in orange scrubs next to his lawyer, who wore a nice suit. It was strange seeing Galvin in something other than his normal attire.

"Seattle County District Zone three, The Honorable Judge Garrett Johnsville will be hearing the testimony here today to determine the verdicts for Galvin Holt in the first Human Trafficking jury trial in this district," said the bailiff in a bored tone.

From here, I could see Galvin giving the judge a displeased look that said more than any words possibly could.

Galvin's lawyer, who had greased back hair, a very pale face, and seemed to be coming down from a high, began with a strong voice. "You are here today because of charges of alleged human and child trafficking, along with charges of assault and kidnapping. Is that correct, Mr. Holt?"

"Correct," Galvin replied, keeping his eyes on the man.

Cory turned back to Galvin. "Mr. Holt, do you know any of the women in these photos?" He laid out a number of pictures on the table.

Galvin considered for only a short moment before denying any knowledge of them.

"What do you plead against the charges after seeing those women?" Cory asked, removing the photos.

"I am innocent. I only admit to selling and buying illegal drugs," Galvin said.

"I'm done," Cory said with a shrug as he made his way back to his seat. Galvin was not pleased by this, as he glared at the man.

"I bet he'll turn up dead by the end of the week," Kaleb mumbled to me. I couldn't agree more.

"Do we have any witnesses?" the judge asked calmly.

"Not at this time, your honor," answered the Assistant District Attorney as he stood.

"Mr. Jake White," the judge said. "Child sex trafficking is a silent in all communities across our nation. The victims of human trafficking suffer long-lasting psychological and physical violence at the hands of their traffickers."

Mr. White had tanned skin and dressed nicely. He was here on behalf of the women who didn't want to face Galvin, as he had caused enough pain.

"Any other questioning?" the judge asked, looking over at Galvin.

"Let us recess, and I will be back with my ruling," the judge said, standing and leaving the courtroom when no one had any more questioning. Galvin continued to sit there, whispering to his lawyer, who was even paler from what he was being told. I halfway felt sorry for the poor druggy.

"Hey," Jake said, turning around to face us, as we sat behind him. "I'm pretty sure Galvin will be held accountable for everything, since he has a very crappy lawyer with him."

"Yeah, I figured he would have had someone better represent him," Kaleb said, leaning forward so their voices wouldn't carry.

"Yeah, I am surprised, but considering how the mafia isn't happy about his choices, I'm really not expecting much from them. The big shots are very against human trafficking. They're the ones who usually bring it down, so if Galvin gets out, he will be killed within hours," Jake said. "He won't even make it in prison." A pause. "Still no word on Morgan?"

"No, nothing," I answered, shaking my head. "He's been keeping an eye on me and my girls, but otherwise, we can't get close to him. He's a step ahead, and he will make a mistake soon."

"Erick Martin was taken and proven guilty easily, so there will be no trial for him. He cried like a baby when his lawyer and detective got his statement," Jake said.

"All rise," said the bailiff as the door opened and the judge entered fifteen minutes later.

DAWN

It was strange, being home without Elijah nearby. Sure, he had left before to run to the store, which would be an hour at the most. This time, he would be gone for at least four hours, possibly more depending on the verdict of the case and how long it would take.

Kelly was with me, keeping me company as our girls played next to each other. I was quieter today, mostly lost in thought. I wasn't worried, knowing Galvin wouldn't be set free. They had more than enough evidence against him to put him away for life.

"So, then, this guy came up to me and was like, acting all hot, when in reality he was *not* that great looking," Kelly said, telling me a story about a college experience she'd had at a frat party. "And you aren't even listening. What's up, Sug?"

"I don't know," I sighed. "I can't shake the feeling something's wrong." I had woken up this morning with a weird feeling.

"I'm sure everything is fine. Kaleb and Elijah should be back this afternoon, if not earlier."

"I don't think it's them. It's something else."

"Like what?" she asked.

"That's just it; I don't know," I said, aggravated.

"Zack is home today, I think. Do you want me to give him a call and see if he can come hang out? Would that help?" Kelly asked.

"No, I'll be fine," I said, shaking my head. I didn't want to bug him if it really wasn't anything. There could be a number of reasons for my feelings.

Pushing it to the back of my mind, I turned my attention to the girls, watching them play.

Lily was now able to sit by herself, and she was slobbering on a toy that played music. The two didn't pay much attention to one another, but as they grew and aged, they would.

It was shortly after we got the girls down for a nap after lunch when the boys arrived back home. Elijah seemed worried, but he schooled his face once he saw me. Kaleb, on the other hand, was fuming with rage.

"Morgan followed us," he said as he took a gentle seat on the couch next to Kelly, who leaned into him. "That little twat. What does he think he's playing at?"

"He's waiting for the time to strike, and we'll be ready," Elijah said, trying to soothe the nerves in the room. I was in his arms instantly, seeking his familiar warmth.

"How long has he been following us?" I asked, looking up at him with worry.

"Weeks. We can't catch him; he seems to be one step ahead. I don't know what he's playing at or trying to accomplish, but we will get him. In the meantime, we'll be staying at home more, just to be safe. I don't truly think he'll try to do anything to get past the gate," Elijah answered. "He's not too bright, but he is smart enough to not push me."

"Do you think maybe he wants to know if Dawn is still staying here? Or wondering if maybe she went to the hearing today with you?" Kelly asked.

"Yeah, it crossed my mind. Of course, Morgan not seeing her with me the last few times I've gone out should give him more than enough to know I'm not taking chances. Maybe I should give him a call, but he may know who I work with," Elijah said.

"I wouldn't call," Kaleb said. "He most likely knows about everything by now. He was bailed out of jail for a reason."

"So, what was the verdict?" Kelly asked, changing the subject.

"Galvin was sentenced life in prison, with no possible parole," Elijah answered, leading me to sit down on the loveseat. "His lawyer was just getting off a high, so he wasn't the best."

"That's putting it mildly," Kaleb laughed.

I was just happy he would no longer be an issue I had to deal with. The lifted weight was refreshing, and I knew things were going to start looking up for us.

CHAPTER 26

ELIJAH

It was now early February, and the snow was packed in force to the sides of the roads. It was just now starting to look like the snow may be done, at least for a few days. With the snow came the frostbiting cold. The wind was the worst, so we didn't go out much due to Lizzy being so little, and I didn't want Dawn getting sick.

Kelly had talked us into letting her keep our Lizzy for a night, saying we were in need of a night to ourselves, but expected us to keep her daughter the following week so she and Kaleb could spend a night alone.

Dawn was full of nerves, which was normal for any first-time mother, to allow her child to stay somewhere without her. We both knew Kelly and Kaleb were more than capable of watching another little one.

It had been a month now since the trial of Galvin. It was big news for days on end, since the reporters couldn't believe that the trail was so short. Most trials last for days, sometimes up to months before a verdict comes down, but with the

193

evidence, and with the victims stepping forward, it was a no-brainer. It was better for us all. It was a plus that the judge didn't want to spend days hearing the same thing over and over.

I wasn't happy when the news leaked our names just a week ago.

"Hey, turn the news on," Kaleb said right after I answered my phone. Dawn was in the shower, and I wanted a show, but I guess that would have to wait.

Turning on the TV, I saw what he was wanting me to see.

"This information has come to us through a secret source. It has been said that the FBI of Seattle has been using an undercover police officer — possibly more than one — to bring down Galvin and his fellow men. His name is Elijah Hunter. We have been unable to locate him at this time to confirm or deny these allegations; nor have we been able to obtain any photographs of him. We have called and left messages with the Chief, Kaleb Morgan, but have not gotten a reply as of yet. We will keep you updated on this as more information becomes available," the newscaster said.

"That's it?" I asked, not at all concerned. They would soon find a death certificate, leading them nowhere.

"Yeah. I'm betting it was Morgan," Kaleb said.

"I'm not worried, Kaleb. He can tell whoever he wants, but he doesn't know my real last name, so he won't be able to lead anyone to me. I already have Tom getting a few more documents in the works," I answered. "And no one can get past my gate without my permission now, since I put that new code on the alarm. If Morgan tried to lead anyone here, Elijah Hunter isn't here."

"No one can find you from your name, anyway. You're not truly a Brown, either," he laughed.

He was correct. I was adopted but chose to keep my last name, adding Hunter to the end. I was Elijah Brown-Hunter.

That was why I used Elijah Hunter for my false documentation while bringing Galvin down. Elijah Brown for work purposes.

Deciding we'd stay in, Dawn and I went to the pool

house. She was nervous about it, but that could easily be because she was wearing her two-piece swimsuit, a huge robe wrapped around her for warmth. The path to the pool house was cleared of snow, but that didn't mean it was any warmer outside.

Dawn wore her hair up in a high bun so it wouldn't get wet. I carried a backpack of a few snacks and water, along with towels. I had a bounce in my step as we made it to the door.

When I opened the white door, the smell of chlorine and warmth hit us, and steam rolled out around us.

"Wow," Dawn said, entering before me. The pool house was completely open except for the bathroom and shower area. To one side, there were a few lounge chairs against the windows that could easily be opened during the summer.

The clean blue pool, which was only five feet deep, sat close to the chairs and was heated all year long. On the other side, there was a hot tub, steam rising from it.

"I don't use them often, but it is nice when I have the time to enjoy it," I said, leading Dawn farther into the room.

She looked around the huge room in awe. I wasn't sure what she was thinking, but I sat the backpack of items down near the chairs.

"Come on," I said, motioning to the pool first while she took off her white robe.

Underneath, I expected the swimsuit she and Kelly had ordered. I didn't expect what she had on. It was a skimpy two piece, a dark red string bikini and hardly covered anything on her. It wouldn't take much for her breasts to spill out. The bottoms were tied on her hips in neat little bows.

"Where did you get that one?" I asked, looking her up and down like I was ready to eat her. I licked my lips, knowing the game she was playing.

"Mandy may have bought it for me," she said, looking up

through her eyelashes at me with a little smirk. "Do you like it?" she asked.

"Very," I said, trying to swallow and will down my erection. I almost had to wonder what had happened to my shy, sweet girl, but with her hanging out with Kelly and Mandy, and sometimes Emily, I was sure they helped my girl figure out ways to try and seduce me. "Come on," I said, stepping into the pool, holding my hand out for her to join me.

After a moment, she gripped my hand tightly and slowly entered the pool with me. She was surprised the water was warm, and she relaxed once it was up to the top of her breasts. They floated up, and I could see her hardened nipples.

"Isn't so bad?" I asked with a smile as I pulled her into a hug.

She shook her head. Her green eyes looked at me with happiness and love.

"Why don't you come in here more often?" she asked, pushing up against me more.

"Well, before you, I threw myself into work. I had nothing to do here at home." I shrugged, enjoying the feeling of her breasts pushed up against me. I could just feel her warmth against my cock. "Now that you're here, I have more reason to come."

"Is that so?" she asked sweetly, tilting her head upwards. I knew she was standing on her tippy toes so the water wouldn't overtake her.

"Yes," I said, right before I met her lips with my own.

Instantly, her lips molded into mine. I moved my right hand up her back to her neck, giving her support as she tilted her head back more. I took advantage of it, swiping my tongue along her mouth, seeking entrance. She opened with a gasp.

My other hand stayed at her waist, playing with the tie of her bottoms.

"Dawn," I panted, breaking the kiss and leaning my forehead against hers, breathing deeply. "You're playing with fire again."

"Am I?" she asked, trying to act coy.

Oh, Dawn, you little minx, I thought. I smiled sweetly at her before pulling her closer to me. She was beginning to test her boundaries, and I was all too happy to help her discover them.

"You certainly are," I said, bending to kiss and nibble her neck, making her squeak in surprise.

After a few minutes with her rubbing her heat along my hardened dick, I told her to hop out and head to the hot tub, where we could sit and relax. While she did that, I dug in the backpack, getting two bottles of water out, along with something special. She was more than ready.

∼

DAWN

I'm not sure when it happened, but I was feeling brave. It could be that I was finally starting to look like a healthy human again, not just skin and bones. I had energy. I kept the house cleaned easily these days, and enjoyed spending time with Elijah and Lizzy and our friends. I wasn't as shy as I once was. I willingly talked, stated my fears, and asked any questions without fear of being yelled at or hit, or shut away in a dark room.

I sat down so the jets set on low relaxed my muscles. It was nice to not feel sore and tired all the time.

He turned on the stereo, and Hozier began to play 'Arsonist's Lullaby'.

"Enjoying the warm water?" Elijah asked, entering the tub and handing me a bottle of water, already opened.

"Yes," I said with a smile before taking a drink. "I could have used this those first few days I was here."

"I didn't know you well, or how you would respond in those days—if it would scare you more or help you. I would have gladly let you come here if I'd known you might like it," he said with a sad look in his eyes.

"I didn't know I wasn't supposed to be sore then," I shrugged, setting my water off to the side. "I thought it was normal."

As we grew quiet, I scooted over so I was sitting right next to him. He sat leaning back with his eyes closed, relaxing. I quickly looked down, seeing his legs stretched out in front of him. Smiling, I reached over, laying my hand on his upper thigh and swirling my fingertips there.

He opened his eyes slowly, looking at me, and moved his own hand to my thigh, copying my movements. I closed my eyes, enjoying the feel of his warm hand on me before opening them and smiling at him shyly. I slowly moved my hand up, covering his hardness and pressing down just a tad, making him to moan.

"Come sit on my lap, back to my front," he said, helping me move so I wouldn't fall. "Do you think you're up to playing with a toy?"

"I don't know," I answered once I was sitting on his lap, his cock pulsing just behind me. He had his hands on my hips, holding me still so I couldn't move. "What kind of toy?" I was curious. I was already wet and ready.

I'd found I liked playing around with Elijah. As I became braver, my needs seem to be more prominent.

"This." He brought out a small waterproof vibrator. It was light pink, and not very long at all. "It's for beginners and has different levels of vibration so we can find out what you like best. If you don't like it, we don't have to use it."

"Okay," I said, looking at the thing. I didn't want to touch it, but I knew my face was bright red at just the thought.

"Many women find them to be quite enjoyable, with more time and more experience. Just because you may not like this one, doesn't mean you won't like something else. They come in many different styles and shapes. This one here is jelly, so it will slip into your pussy easily, and feel closest to a real dick," Elijah said. He laid it down on the edge of the hot tub before pulling me back more against his chest and gently moving my head so it lay against his shoulder.

He began to kiss me along my neck, his hands slowly making their way gently down my arms. I kept my breaths even, enjoying the feeling.

He then brought them back up to my breasts, massaging them through the material of my swim suit. I moaned lightly, arching into him for more.

He gently pushed my swimsuit up and over my breasts, letting them float in the water as he tweaked the nipples, making them both hard.

"Are you wet for me yet?" he asked huskily.

"I have been since we came in."

"Oh, you have, have you?" he said, slipping the ties around my bottoms undone on one side, then the other, before rubbing my mound through the fabric.

"Yes," I moaned, arching my hips upwards, trying to seek much-needed friction.

"I see," he hummed, removing his hands from me to lower his own trunks.

Once he was situated again, he grabbed the vibrator and ran it down my body, from my breasts to my pussy. It wasn't on yet; he was getting my body used to the feeling of it.

"Let me know if you need me to stop," he breathed as he turned the vibrator to the lowest setting as it sat on my inner thigh. It sort of tickled, but I stayed still as his hand began to roughly squeeze my breast.

"Yes, Sir," I said with a deep breath. I lifted my hands and wrapped them around his neck, pulling him even closer.

Even slower, he moved the vibrator to my outer lips, being careful of putting any pressure on me there. After a short moment, he moved it up, hitting my clit, making me to moan out and arch upwards.

"So responsive," he said, watching me and my reactions closely. "You like it."

"More, please, Sir," I begged in a breathy voice.

He moved it down, inserting just the thin tip, and I could feel it all through my body. Slowly, he pushed it in, letting me get used to the feeling. It was warmed by the water and smaller than Elijah was, but it still felt good. Almost too good. It wouldn't take much more for me to be pushed over the edge.

He turned it up another notch. I gasped in shock as the wave of pleasure increased, warming my lower belly even more. His hand on my breast switched sides as he began to thrust the vibrator in and out, slowly, and not allowing it to hit my clit or g-spot.

Before I could blink, he removed the device and moved me up just a little, where his pulsing cock slid right into me.

"Ohh," I moaned out, not expecting the sensation of being full so soon. I felt him throb inside me, and my walls wrapped around him, squeezing him tightly. I would never tire of him entering me. He was warm, and all man.

"You are still so dang fucking tight," he grunted out, slowly moving me up and down.

With him inside me this way, he hit spots I didn't know were there. I couldn't help but moan loudly as he pushed upwards again.

"I'm so close," I managed to pant as he began to move faster, making my breasts bounce against the water, splashing it over the edges.

"Me too," he groaned. He moved one hand to my clit, pinching and rubbing, while the other pulled my hardened nipple.

I cried out, my walls squeezing around him. He came, hard, squirting his cum, warming me even more.

We sat there, both catching our breaths, basking in the warmth and the connection we shared. Lately, every time he touched me—even just a little touch—my skin sparked, igniting with fire. He was meant to be mine, and me his. We were one.

CHAPTER 27

ELIJAH

I wasn't sure about this, but Dawn was asking for it, both with her voice and her body. She had been teasing me again all morning while we worked in the kitchen and the rest of the house. I swear she wore those too-tight yoga pants and try to kill me. Every time she'd bend over, I could see she had no underwear on, and I was hard instantly. I tried to tame my thoughts, but it didn't work—not with such a vixen teasing me endlessly.

The day before, we had gone to the doctor's office for Dawn to have a complete checkup, along with Lizzy. Dawn had mentioned wanting to know if she was able to carry children if we chose to later. With our daughter still so young, we didn't want one right away, but I was thrilled Dawn was thinking about it. More than thrilled, actually.

If she did have any issues that were fixable, we wanted to take the steps now while we could, and not be in a hurry to do so later when we knew we wanted more. I'm not sure what her doctor told her, but she came out all smiles. Dawn wouldn't let me in there, which I could understand. I didn't need to be, but would have if she'd asked. I had to guess that whatever they talked about, it was good.

I was thrilled Dawn could be in a doctor's office without me in her sight, showing me she was healing—moving on from the tragic life she had been forced to live.

"Do you want more children, Elijah?" Dawn asked as we were enjoying a movie late one afternoon. The sun was shining through the window while Lizzy played with a few of her toys on the floor close by. She was getting big way too fast.

"If you want to, absolutely," I had answered, looking at her with my entire attention

"I think I do," she mused aloud. "I mean, I didn't ever think I would be able to have one after the one I lost, but with Elizabeth, I can see me having at least one."

"We can try, at least. If you can't, we can adopt," I answered. I didn't mind adopting one bit. We had already adopted Lizzy, and it wouldn't take much to adopt another—or two.

Lizzy was growing, gaining weight like a normal baby would. She was behind in a few motor skills, but it wasn't anything to worry about. She was six months old and was now just able to sit up by herself, but she was the happiest baby we could have asked for. She fussed a little with teething but she had yet to get sick, which was good considering she was so small at birth. Lilly had gotten a nasty cold shortly after Christmas, and I had worried Lizzy would catch it, but she never did.

Lizzy had left with my mother, having a girl's day, and Dawn had been set on teasing me all morning. I couldn't help but pounce on her when the moment came.

She had just shut the front door when I pinned her up against it, grabbing her hands and pinning them above her head. She lightly squeaked in fright before relaxing against me with a smug smile.

"Are you trying to test me?" I whispered near her ear, pushing my hard cock into her core.

"No, Sir," she answered all too sweetly with a smug smile still in place. She pushed back against me, almost making me to moan. Swallowing, I moved back a step, still keeping Dawn pinned to the door. I looked her up and down, imagining her naked and sprawled out before me. I could see her bent over the couch, or my desk, with her ass sticking out, waiting for me.

"Are you really sure you want to do this?" I asked, keeping my voice calm and collected, letting her take control for the moment, but also letting my Dom voice come out. I knew she would never allow me to be her Master, and I was okay with that.

"Absolutely, Sir," Dawn replied, going straight into sub mode, but not dropping her eyes from my own. My cock twitched.

"I'll give you one more chance," I said, letting go of her hands. I knew this was coming, but I wasn't sure if she was up to it yet, or if she really knew what was expected. "If this is what you want, I will be more than happy to oblige, but if not, you have to let me know *now* before we go any further, Dawn."

Instead of replying, she kneeled in front of me in the most perfect pose I could ever ask for. She had her hands, palms down, on her bent knees. Her hair was tied back in a simple braid which fell over her shoulder, and she kept her head down. Her knees were only an inch apart.

I couldn't wait to see her in other waiting positions, but not today.

"I am here to please you, Sir," she said in a low voice filled with lust. She remained in position, not moving other than to breathe.

"I want you naked, kneeling by the bed within three minutes," I said, thinking of which toys to bring down from my playroom, hoping I was making the right decision on this. I was afraid it was too soon, but she was in an overly good mood today, so hopefully she wouldn't have any issues.

Without saying a word, Dawn stood and made her way upstairs. I could hear her soft footsteps once she reached the landing.

Giving her some time to both strip and make sure her thoughts were on what was to come, I made my way to the playroom.

With a deep breath, I grabbed a silk rope, and the smallest butt plug, along with some lube, just to see what she should do. I wasn't sure I would even use either of them on her at this time. Whips were out of the question. I don't think I could bring myself to ever use them on her.

Making my way back downstairs, I entered the bedroom. There, by the bed, kneeled my girl in the same way she had taken downstairs, but naked. Setting the items down on the side dresser, I began to strip my clothes. I could hear Dawn's breathing pick up as I unzipped my pants, and I couldn't help but smile at her reaction.

"What color are you?" I asked, taking off my boxers.

"Green, Ma . . . Sir," she said.

"If you would like, you can all me Sir, or Mr. Brown," I said, giving the option. I loved the way *Master* almost fell from her lips just moments earlier.

"Sir," she said with a sexy smile, glancing up at me through her eyelashes.

"I am very pleased with you, kitten," I said, running the pad of my finger along her cheek. I could see my praise was much needed, as her face brightened instantly. "Now." I lifted her head up with my finger under her chin. "I want my cock in your mouth."

Without any prompts, she licked the tip, making me hiss before she took me halfway in. Without any foreplay, she sucked on me, making me to moan deep in my throat. She was testing my control, and we had only just started.

"Slower," I ground out, tangling my hands in her hair, not caring if it got messed up.

She slowed, licking the underside of my cock, right along the vein. I wanted to pound into her warm wet mouth, but held myself back, letting her tease me, bringing me to the edge before I pulled her head back by her hair. I took a small step back from her. This wasn't about my pleasure.

"Up on the bed. Lie on your back," I demanded.

It didn't take her long before she lay there—still, but not as relaxed.

"Color?" I asked, walking up to her and rubbing her legs up and down.

"Yellow," she said, closing her eyes.

"Can you tell me why?" I asked, needing to know what was going on in her mind.

She took a deep breath before opening her eyes, meeting my own. "I'm okay," she said, not answering my question.

"Are you sure?" I asked. I wasn't going to proceed if she wasn't one hundred percent sure. I knew there would be times she would get lost in her thoughts, and wouldn't be able to get through any scenes. I knew I should demand more of an explanation from her, but I didn't want to ruin the mood.

"Yes," she hissed, drawing my attention to her. She had her hands down by her sides, holding onto the blanket for dear life. Her eyes filled with fear, but also determination. I could tell right away something was wrong, and I refused to allow her to push herself like this. Yes, it was always wonderful to see a sub push through any fear, but with Dawn's history, I wouldn't allow it—not today.

"I call red," I said, sitting down by her waist. Her eyes filled with tears and she shook her head.

"Please, no," she cried, trying to turn her body away from me.

"Dawn," I said, wrapping my arms around her from behind, my erection softening as I did what I could to soothe my girl. I hated her tears, but it was a healing process. It always would be.

∼

DAWN

I thought I could handle it. I don't know why my past had to come out right then, when I was fine just minutes earlier. I wanted to please him, to bring him to the edge of sensation like he had done for me countless of times. Sure, we had a few nights where we were both satisfied, but I was ready for more—or at least I thought I was. My needs were stronger and growing every day. When I looked at him, I wouldn't help but want more of him in every way.

"I want you on that bed," the man said.

I slowly lay on the bed, hoping he'd just get it done and over with. My ribs were tender, and so were my legs from the last client. The hallways and other rooms were quiet, as it was earlier than normal to perform services. I didn't think anything of it, as it had happened a few times here and there.

I hated the quiet, and that alone made me feel on edge. I could see Galvin standing in the doorway with a pleased look on his face as the man above me rammed his dick into me none too gently.

Tears gathered in my eyes; I was dry as a desert but didn't voice anything. Apparently, the man didn't like that, as he moved his hands up to my neck and put pressure against me, making black spots appear.

"Shh, Dawn, I got you," Elijah said, soothing me as he held me from behind.

"Music, please," I sobbed out, needing something other than the quiet of the room.

"Of course," Elijah said, moving and leaning over the bed to get his phone. It was only a moment later when Iron and Wine began to play that I slowly relaxed, letting Elijah's hold calm me some.

After a few moments, when my breathing was calmer and the tears had dried, Elijah spoke. "What happened?"

"It was too quiet," I answered simply and quietly. "I can't do the quiet, I guess."

"Okay. I'll make sure to put music on if you ever want to do that again, before anything else," he agreed easily. "Music can also enhance the enjoyment."

"I'm sorry," I said sadly, turning around to face him. His arms never left me, hugging me close to him. "I really wanted to play. I want to show you that I can be the sub you need." I was more upset at myself than anything.

"There's nothing to be sorry for," he said, kissing me on the head. "It will take time, and I don't need you doing my every command. I have loved what we have been able to do." He paused. "And you're perfect the way you are."

"I should be able to," I huffed out, burying my face against his bare chest.

"You will, in time. We have to work slow, take one step at a time before leaping," Elijah soothed me. "You will get there. It's a process, and with what you went through, I don't expect you to be able to just jump right in. I'm happy that you even want to try, and that's what counts."

"I love you," I sighed, looking up at him.

"I love you too," he replied before gently kissing my lips.

I felt off and upset at myself. I didn't know what to do, but I knew Elijah was right. I had to give it time. Maybe the next time we had a few hours to ourselves, we could try again. Or, maybe Kelly and Kaleb's offer still stood—I could watch them do a scene, so I knew what to expect.

We ended up falling asleep, hanging onto one another. Elijah was up first, letting me sleep longer as he took a shower and got the room picked up the room before I ever got up. I found him naked, just getting out of the shower when I entered.

Not able to help myself, I took his soft dick in my hand, enjoying the feel. I felt smug when he grew and groaned, leaning his head against the top of my head.

"If you start, you have to finish it," he muttered happily.

I was more than happy to, bringing him a fast relief before taking a shower myself.

Once we were both ready, we headed out to pick up Lizzy from Joslyn. She could have easily brought her home, but Elijah said he needed to get out of the house for just a few minutes, so we both decided to go.

The late March sky was overcast with dark clouds from the incoming storm that was to bring us a few inches of snow and slick, icy roads. It wasn't predicted to start snowing until late that night, so we had plenty of time

"Can you get your phone and put it in your socks?" Elijah asked, glancing up at the rearview mirror again. He kept looking at them more often than usual.

I did as he said, digging my phone from my purse and sticking it in my sock, keeping it safely hidden. I hardly ever turned it on, since anyone who wanted to get hold of me called Elijah. I always tended to leave my phone either in my purse or in the bedroom, except when Elijah went out. I gave him a look—he was stiff and on edge.

"There's someone following us," he said, taking a turn along a different street. "I don't know what they're up to, but I'm not leading them to my mother's house."

I looked behind us, seeing a black car following.

Picking up his own phone, he called Kaleb, telling him where we were and to track the car's location as he took turns that led us away from his parents. He slowly sped up, increasing his speed. His voice was rough with nerves, and possibly thrill. He was an FBI agent, and from what I had seen on TV, they liked the feel of the chase; but usually, the rules were reversed.

"I'm going to take you back home and have Joslyn keep Lizzy," Elijah said, taking a sharp turn around a corner as the car behind us caught up.

"Who is it?" I asked, not sure if wanted to know the answer.

"Morgan," Elijah answered, sending a bolt of fear down my spine. "Hang on."

There wasn't really much to hang onto, as he turned another corner, peeling out as the back tires screeched before he gunned it again, going down a different road. I gripped the handle on the door with one hand, and with the other, I grabbed onto the seat belt as I was roughly forced to the side as he turned the corner. Both my hands were white as I held on for what felt like my life.

Once he got the car straightened out, another came out of the trees fast, hitting us on the front fender sideways, making us to swerve off the road and into a ditch, rolling once. My head hit the side door window. We were going too fast for Elijah to brake safely to try to slow the collision.

The airbags blew, hitting me in the face and blocking my vision from the front and side. Everything began to blur together.

The sound of the front window breaking reached my ears with the impact as the car rolled on its side. The roof gave in against the ground. There was a thud as the other side flipped over. The car bounced, once, twice, before stopping, motionless. My heart pounded, and I could feel a trickle of blood down the side of my face.

The last thing I heard before everything went dark was Elijah.

"Shit!"

CHAPTER 28

ELIJAH

I woke up with a pounding headache, my face smashed up against the steering wheel, and a blood smeared air bag. I heard sirens off in the distance, but no other sounds. It was too quiet in the car.

Slowly, I pushed myself so I was sitting, trying to figure out what had happened and where I was.

I could feel warm blood dripping down my arm where glass cut into my skin. A sweet-smelling odor from the engine reached me.

I needed to move.

Now.

Looking over to the passenger seat, I saw the door was open and Dawn was nowhere in sight. It had to have been opened from the outside as it was caved inward from the impact. The glass was completely shattered, sharp pieces sticking up where it used to be in the frame.

Surprisingly, the car had landed on its deflated tires after doing a full roll. My body felt sore from the impact already.

Steam was rising out of the engine, and I forced myself to unbuckle and crawl out the open door. I could feel the small pieces of glass cutting into my palms and knees.

"Dawn!" I yelled. My head began to pound more, but I ignored it. I kept yelling for Dawn.

I don't know how long I screamed for her, but once my brain realized she wasn't here, I collapsed, gasping for breath as the sirens grew louder, before voices and movement reached my senses. I couldn't move as tears poured down my face, crouching there on the ground. I kneeled, hunched over, gasping for breath, still calling for my girl as loud as I could, my voice growing hoarse. I think I puked, as the sour smell reached my nose.

"I'll get him; check the car." I heard Kaleb's voice as he pushed his way to me. "Elijah?" he said, drawing my attention to him.

"She's gone," I cried out, looking at him. "I have to find her." I went to stand, but my legs gave out. Kaleb caught me and helped me walk to the ambulance before he said anything. I couldn't think of anything but finding my girl.

"I'll find her," he said, helping me to lay back on the cot so the medics could strap me in. "I'll meet you at the hospital, okay?"

Everything seemed to be fog covered and I didn't know what to do. I had never panicked before. Not when Dawn was taken the first time. Not when I had lost my mentor to another. Not when I couldn't get a case right at work.

"Kaleb," I managed to say, before I blacked out in panic, letting the darkness be a promise for hope, for calm.

∼

Beep. Beep. Beep.

Slowly, I came back to consciousness. I could feel each bruise, each cut and mark on my body. I could feel the IV in my right hand, pushing fluids into my sore body. My eyes refused to open. Now I had an idea of how Dawn must have felt when she first came to me.

It was pure hell.

I knew I was in a hospital. It wasn't often I ended up in one, so I knew it must be pretty bad. I remembered why I was here and grimaced at the thought.

Groaning, I forced my heavy eyes open, but shut them instantly. The light above me was too bright. Way too fucking bright.

"Elijah?" I heard my mother whisper out softly, and a soft touch on my other hand. I squeezed, letting her know I was awake.

"Oh, Elijah," she cried out, laying her head over our hands.

"Mom?" I blinked my eyes open, expecting the extremely bright light this time. I had to blink a few times to clear my vision.

"I was so worried about you," she said, but it came out muffled. "You've been asleep for hours."

"Where's . . . Where's . . .?" I managed to get out before the beeping of the heart monitor began to rise, showing my panic.

"Shh. Lizzy's with Kelly," Mom said.

"Dawn?" I breathed out in panic. I could see the black dots in my vision. "Where is she?" I could feel my heartbeat through my entire body, racing. Faster. Faster.

Thump. Thump. Thump.

"You have to calm down, please," my mom begged as a nurse flew in the room with a needle. She inserted whatever drug into my system through the IV, and I felt the effects almost immediately. They calmed me, relaxing me, making me fall asleep.

"Get Kaleb," I managed to mumble out before darkness covered me once again. I tried to fight it, but it was useless.

KALEB

I was seething. Beyond seething, if it was possible. I couldn't believe that little dick got an up on us, yet again. He was going to meet my fist—and more—when I tracked the fucker down this time. I wasn't the reasonable FBI Chief now; I should have killed that bastard on site. I still might, anyway —consequences be damned.

I knew I should have moved Elijah and Dawn to a different location. It was plain as day that Morgan was watching their every move. I didn't know what he had planned, but I was pretty dang sure he was after the girl who was like a baby sister to me.

She had changed Elijah for the better. Elijah had always thrown himself into his work, even at such a young age. He wasn't ever really happy with how his life was going, but he did the best he could. He was lonely and angry most of the time—until Dawn came back into his life.

When I first met him, he was alone, sitting at the bar looking around. That had been a few years ago. I couldn't help but reach out to him—in more than one way. I've always swung both ways, and I found him to be attractive, in a bad boy kind of way.

He wore all black, including a leather jacket. He seemed lost, not sure of anything. His body was stiff, but he was searching for something, most likely a one-night stand. He was new to this area, or at least to this bar.

"Hey, cowboy," I greeted, as I walked up next to him, ordering a stiff drink.

"Oh, uh, hey?" he said, confused. His bright blue eyes were clouded with indecision. His dark blond hair touched his chin. I couldn't wait to run my fingers through it.

"Come to let some steam off tonight?" I asked, letting my eyes

roam up and down. He wasn't the usual type I'd try to hit on, but I could see he wasn't sure about what he liked. Why not give it shot, right?

Normally, I'd never go for someone who had no clue about my lifestyle. I liked the easy prey who seemed to always be lining up for me.

"I guess so," *he simply shrugged, turning back around to ask for a water. I looked him over, wondering his age. If I had to take a guess, I would say he was about twenty, maybe.*

"Girl trouble?" *I couldn't help but ask, wanting to know what was going on inside that head of his. I had to make sure that he, in fact, was single.*

"I wish," *he sighed, running a hand through his hair.* "I can't stand any of the girls I've met lately."

"Then what has you so stressed?" *I asked, leaning into his personal space just a tad.*

"Life," *he sighed.*

"So, what are you planning to do here tonight, then?" *I asked, indicating his water.* "You not of drinking age?"

"I can try to find a nice person older than me to order my drinks," *he winked with a laugh.* "Then hope to get laid."

"Well, I can help you with both," *I winked back, watching as his face freeze before he turned bright red.*

"What?" *he stuttered, once he got his thoughts back in order.* "I . . . I don't. . . do guys," *he said, but I could hear and see the idea was almost appealing to him. His voice wasn't as deep as some men I'd had relations with. Plus, I'm pretty sure he'd just tried to flirt with me.*

"Are you sure about that?" *I asked with a sweet smile his way* "You seem the type to be up for trying new things."

It didn't take him long to find out what he wanted. I was easy on him that first time, giving him a wonderful blow job and getting one in return. That was the night we became good friends—and more. But what we had wasn't love, it was a way for him to grow, to figure out what he wanted and needed out of life.

I knew I should have been there with him in the hospital since he was so distraught after the crash, and with Dawn missing again for the second time in his life. I couldn't blame him. She was the light of his life.

I was at the station, trying to track her phone, but it didn't seem to be giving us a signal. I knew time was not on our side, and I had no idea where Morgan had taken her. I just hoped she'd find a way to get a message to us, or to try to run. We had many of our guys out looking every single place we possibly could.

Joslyn called later the next morning, saying that Elijah had woken up in a panic again and that I needed to be there the next time he did. She didn't know what to do. He needed to be calm so I could get him out of there and to a safe house in case Morgan came back and tried to finish him off.

When I had got to him, he had been covered in blood, with a few deep cuts from the glass. He had a good bruise across his forehead and down his face. I was sure Morgan would have taken him out if given the choice, but since Dawn was there, he took her instead.

The car hit Dawn's side—hard. It had been stolen, and the driver was nowhere to be found. I was worried about what sort of state she would be in, and hoped she could get away from Morgan sooner rather than later, or that we could figure out where he was.

I was tired but knew I couldn't go home. I called Kelly, letting her know I was going to wait for Elijah to wake up again at the hospital, since he was sedated. I hoped he wouldn't panic as much if I was there.

Once I got to the hospital, I nodded to the police officer standing outside his room before entering. Joslyn sat in what looked like the most uncomfortable white chair next to the bed, looking around the room as she tried to stay awake.

Elijah lay in the hospital bed, eyes closed as he slept. A white blanket covered him up to his armpits, with his arms laid out over the top. The blood had been cleaned off him, and the cuts were stitched. I'm sure he hurt like a bitch.

"Go home," I said, patting her shoulder. "Or at least go rest in Vence's office and lie down. I'll call you when he wakes."

"Thanks, Kaleb," she said, standing up and giving me a strong hug. She was worn out and worried. We all were.

I took a seat in her chair and stretched out, waiting for my best friend, once lover, to wake up. I had once promised him I would take care of him no matter what. I wasn't going to break my promise now.

CHAPTER 29

DAWN

I wasn't sure if my eyes were open or closed. Everything was dark. My body was sore and I couldn't move my hands from above my head.

I tried to move the rest of my body, but pain shot up from my feet to my legs—everywhere. I cried out in fear and pain. I moved my head to one side, then the other; I couldn't see anything. I was pretty sure my eyes were open. Had I been blinded in the accident?

"Elijah?" I called out, hoping for an answer. My voice was weak.

I was lying down on something hard, but it wasn't cold like the ground. I hadn't been thrown from the car—at least, I didn't think I had been.

I faintly remembered being pulled from the car by rough hands. They were hands I was used to, and they were not gentle. I heard grunting and someone talking in a German accent but I couldn't make out what was said, or by whom. I couldn't get my mind to move my body. I was helpless.

"Elijah!" I called out again, louder this time as panic began to set in. I pulled on my arms, trying to get them unstuck. It felt like my wrists were tied with a thin rope, cutting the circulation off. "Help!"

I kept yelling, pleading for Elijah, anyone, to help me. My voice grew hoarse before the darkness and the pain took over my body once again.

∾

OPENING MY EYES SOME TIME LATER, I COULD SEE THE MORNING sunshine through a flimsy, dirty curtain. It was a dull light, coating everything in a haze around the small room.

There wasn't much to it. One door was to the right of me, and a small four drawer dresser stood next to me, out of reach.

I couldn't see what my hands were tied with as they were still up above my head. I could hardly feel them. I was lying on a dirty green mattress. There were no blankets, and I wore the same clothes I had on when I left the house. At least knowing I still had clothes on was a relief.

The room smelt dusty, almost musty in a way. It seemed like no one had used the room, possibly this house, for a long time.

Flopping my head back down, I sighed. I had no idea where I was or when I would be let loose. I had no idea what time it was. Would I die here?

I must have dozed off, as I was woken up when the lock turned in the door. I stayed still, faking sleep. The door slowly squeaked open, inch by inch. I leveled out my breathing, even if it meant I wouldn't be free of the rope on my hands anytime soon.

The heavy footsteps carried whoever it was towards me. When the person was close enough to the mattress, he kicked the edge of it, hitting my foot in the process. I jerked but kept my eyes closed and breathing even. I didn't trust him; I didn't even know who it was.

"Still out," he said loudly as he stomped out. His voice was scratchy and deep. It was not someone I knew, nor did it sound like someone I'd had to please before.

"How much did you give her, anyway?" I heard Morgan say from near the door.

"Enough," the man replied. I could picture him shrugging like it wasn't a big deal.

"Whatever," Morgan sighed. "Get lost."

"Got it boss," he said, all too happy to oblige. "Still don't know what you want with her. She's nothing."

"I said get lost, Paul!" Morgan seethed a banging sound reached my ears.

"*Ich werde,*" he mumbled before stomping away, slamming a door a few seconds later. Morgan groaned before entering the room.

His footsteps were softer but his breathing was heavier, for a reason I couldn't guess.

"Oh, my pretty girl. Look at what I had to do," he sighed, bending down so he was closer to me. I felt him brush some of the hair off my face. "I didn't plan to cause you any harm, but I had to have you."

He sighed again. I could feel his eyes on me, looking me over. I wasn't sure what he was looking at, but I had a pretty good idea.

"Oh, for the love of . . ." I heard my mother mumble as she passed the doorway. She stomped angrily away before returning.

"What are you doing, Joan?" Morgan asked with worry.

"Waking her up," she answered hotly, before dumping water on top of my face.

Spluttering and crouching, I opened my eyes. I tried to sit up, forgetting my arms were tied way too tight for me to be able to move at all. The water was ice cold, but at least it halfway cleaned my face of the dried blood.

"See?" Joan said proudly.

Still spluttering, I glanced over at the couple with hatred. I loathed them both for so many reasons. Joan looked tired and much thinner than when I had last seen her. Her bare arms were covered in needle marks from her heroin addiction.

Morgan seemed fairly put together. His face was clean-shaven and he wore what looked to be clean clothes, unlike Joan. He did seem paler than he had been the last time I saw him. Sickly pale.

I remained quiet, waiting to see what would happen. After a few moments, Joan huffed out a breath and stormed out of the room. She slammed things around in another part of the house.

I tugged on the rope again, knowing it was futile, but I didn't know what to do. I felt lost and awkward as Morgan stared at me, not saying anything.

"Sorry 'bout that," he said towards the rope that binded me. "I can't have you running off while I was sleepin'. We won't be here long; it's just a short stop while we rest. I'll be getting rid of her shortly."

"Why?" I asked, deciding I'd try to keep him talking. Maybe I'd try to get him to earn my trust before I tried to escape his hold. I had to get out. I didn't know what he'd do to me, and I couldn't stay here. I was worried about Elijah, and about my baby girl. My mind was going a mile a minute, and I didn't know what to think.

"Why what?" he asked, tilting his head. "Why get rid of your mother?"

"Yeah," I answered. I wanted to know why about a lot of things. Why was I here? Why did he take me?

"Oh, she's always been in the way," he laughed. "A means to an end," he shrugged. "I don't need her. I did in the beginning. She helped get rid of Quentin; he was always around, saying he was going to take you far away. Away from her, away from me. I got her hooked on the heroin, and she couldn't stop. She tried once she knew her debt was paid, but it was so easy to get her to go back to it. Now she only cares about her next hit, it makes it easier on me. Plus, the drugs make her forget things and not care about what she's lost."

"Why me?" I asked, pulling on my arms again, trying to get some sort of feeling back into them.

"Because you are mine," he answered with a smile. "I've never been able to have kids. I tried—with Joan in fact, before she even got pregnant with you—but yeah, it didn't work out. So, I did the next best thing: I killed your dad so I could step in."

"Why did you take me to Galvin, then?" I asked quietly, keeping my emotions out of my voice.

"Joan owed him money. Plus, I was mostly living there and I wanted you trained to be the best of the best. I didn't realize how much I wanted you until then."

"Oh," I said, not really knowing what to say to that. The only thought that went through my head was that he was sick, and needed major help.

"Enough of the talk," Joan shouted through the house.

Groaning, Morgan stood up, giving me another look before he turned.

"Can I use the bathroom, please?" I asked before he left the room. I did need to go, but also wanted to take a look around the house to see if there was any way I could get out.

"Fine," he said, taking a deep breath. "Make it fast. And don't try anything. Got it?"

I nodded. I wouldn't try anything—yet. "Of course."

He carefully untied the rope from its hook on the wall, but not my hands. He smiled sadly at me as he helped me stand. It was a good thing, since I couldn't support myself; my legs were weak. He only laughed as he helped me out of the room and across the hall to the bathroom.

Darn, I was hoping to get a better look. I glanced around and saw a small living room, but that was it, before I was forced into the tiny bathroom.

"I'll leave you be, but I'll be just outside this door," Morgan warned, helping me lean against the stained sink.

Once he was out of sight, I did my business. The bathroom made me cringe as I'd become used to having a clean one. After flushing, I looked in the smoke covered mirror, seeing my reflection.

Part of my face was red and swollen, and a partially dried cut was along my right eyebrow. I ignored the rest of my body as it ached, and I didn't want the visual to go with the pain.

I checked to make sure that the phone was still in my sock before calling out for Morgan. I wasn't going to risk letting him know I had it on me.

"All done?" he asked, too sweetly.

"Yes," I answered, hoping to please him and not say too much. I needed to hide the phone before he tried anything. "Do I have to be tied up again?"

"I guess not. You're weak," he laughed. "Jay not feeding you well enough?"

"No," I simply answered.

"I'll give you something for the pain, okay, child?" Morgan said as he gently sat me back down on the bed.

"You don't have to," I said, not wanting to pass up any moment I could use to call Elijah—as long as my phone worked. I hoped it was charged enough to still make a call.

"I will," he replied. "It's my job to take care of you. I can't have you tired and sore while I enjoy your company." With that, he walked out, leaving the door wide open. I quickly removed the phone from my sock, hiding it under the mattress by my head with shaky hands. I managed to lie down on my side before he came back in, carrying a syringe.

"It'll help, my child," he said, injecting it into my shoulder.

"Now, sleep. I have plans for when you wake." With a kiss to my lips, which I didn't respond to, he left, gently closing the squeaky door behind him. I was asleep before it clicked shut.

~

ELIJAH

The next time I woke up, it was light outside and I groaned as I tried to move. I was uncomfortable all over. Not just painful, but achy. It was quiet; the beeping of the heart machine was the only sound to be heard.

My eyes were caked closed, because I'd been forced to sleep by drugs. I hated drugs for this very reason: it made it hard to think; hard to focus. Giving up on trying to force my eyes open, I let my head relax back against the pillow. I wanted my own bed, my house, and my girls.

I was calmer, and I forced myself to stay that way. I didn't want to be sedated again. I had to get out. I had to find Dawn. Taking a deep breath, I listened around me, hoping something could get my mind off my worries and fears.

I heard breathing from the chair next to the bed and figured it was my mom. She would stay here until I was released, most likely, and then either be at my house or trying to get me to go hers. I just wanted to be left alone, or be teaming up with Kaleb to find my girl.

A snore brought me out of my thoughts, and I couldn't help but smile a little. I knew that snore. Turning my head and forcing my eyes open, I saw Kaleb sitting there, legs spread out and head leaning against the back of the chair. I had to wonder how long he'd been here, and how long I'd been asleep.

There was a light tap on the door before it was pushed open, revealing a nurse. I watched her, not really having anything to say. I wanted to go home, and I'd do just about anything so I could.

"Good morning," she greeted quietly, as she checked the monitors and my chart at the end of the bed. She wore dull blue scrubs. Her black hair was piled high on her head in a messy bun. Her face was rounded and clear of blemishes. She would have been the type I'd have gone for in the past, but since finding Dawn, I didn't want to think about another.

"Mornin'," I replied, my voice quiet and hoarse.

"How are you feeling?" she asked, looking me over with light gray eyes.

"Just dandy," I managed to get out. I felt like I'd been hit by a semi. Every nerve was tainted with pain.

"I'll get you more pain reliever," she smiled kindly, but quietly, as to not wake my guest up. "The doctor should be in shortly."

She left, leaving the door open before returning just a minute later with water and a little white cup containing pain meds.

"Here you go," she said sweetly, looking me over.

"Thanks," I responded before downing them, not caring what they were. I just wanted to feel un-dead, if possible. I sure hoped Dawn was better off, wherever she may be. I had no idea how she'd been able to live with this sort of pain day after day at that prison.

"The pain meds should kick in shortly, and most likely make you groggy, but if you need anything, push the call button, alright?" she said, turning to leave. I simply nodded, too tired and sore to respond.

I laid my head back down against the pillow, letting my eyes close, even though I knew sleep was the furthest thing from my mind. I heard Kaleb move but I kept my eyes closed. He sighed and moved again.

"Damn chair," he grumbled out, shifting again. I couldn't help but laugh as I slowly opened my eyes. I could feel the drugs taking effect, my body becoming lighter. "Elijah?" he asked.

"Yeah," I said, turning my head towards him. He looked tired, like he hadn't gotten a wink of sleep. "They gave me drugs." I smiled at him.

"I can tell," he laughed. "I told the doctor to make sure they didn't give you anything but Advil, but apparently they didn't listen." A pause. "How are you feeling?"

"Like I want to fly," I mumbled out, closing my eyes again. Could I fly? *Where* could I fly?

"Oh, Elijah," Kaleb mumbled. "I'll be right back. Stay," he said, giving me a look I wouldn't ever disobey. Did he really think I would move from this bed? He left and I closed my eyes, thinking about flying. I wondered if I could grow wings. Could I fly to my Dawn, my pretty Dawn, who was not here with me? Where was she? I faintly heard the heart monitor pick up speed as my panic increased yet again.

"Dawn!" I yelled, hoping, praying for her to respond. I had to find her. "Dawn!?"

"Elijah," I heard Kaleb say, and a pressure against my face from his palm. "You have to calm down. They can't sedate you again."

"Kaleb?" I asked, confused. I was looking for Dawn, so why was he here?

"Take a deep breath for me, Elijah," Kaleb said, leaning his forehead against my own. "Like this. In. Out."

I copied him, not knowing why I had to. I was sure my eyes were wide with questions.

"Good," Kaleb praised as my heart began to slow, beating a more normal rhythm. "Again."

"Where am I?" I asked once I was calmer.

"You're in a hospital, and you have to stay calm for me, alright?"

"Oh," I answered confused. "Why?"

"You were in a car accident," he answered. His brown eyes held something that he wasn't telling me.

"I'm tired, Kaleb," I said, letting my eyes close before I quickly opened them again. I felt like I was missing something.

"You can sleep," he said, brushing the hair off my forehead. "I have someone I need to go talk to. Sleep."

"Okay," I mumbled, letting sleep take my body over.

∼

KALEB

"He is not allowed to have any more drugs of any kind. Got it?" I seethed at the attending doctor. I was not thrilled at all about what the nurse had given him. It was meant to help his pain, not make him high as a kite.

I couldn't deny that I sort of enjoyed seeing Elijah high from pain meds, since I'd never seen him like that before. He never once touched any type of drugs, unless they were prescribed by a doctor, and he still wouldn't touch them unless he absolutely needed them.

After scaring the shit out of his doctor, I made a few phone calls, calling in a favor for a new doctor who would know Elijah as well as I did, so no more drugs would be prescribed unless I gave the okay to do so.

I knew when he woke up, he'd either still be high, or cranky as hell. I wasn't sure which would be better; I'd talk him down, either way.

CHAPTER 30

DAWN

I was thankful Morgan had kindly untied my hands, letting me see the rope burns that were left behind. My body was still sore and weak, but it was getting better. The drugs were still in my system, but at least it leveled out the pain for the moment. I felt lightheaded, dizzy in a way. Everything seemed to be spinning around me and I couldn't focus on just one thing.

Morgan was watching something on TV as he sat on the couch next to me while Joan was slamming things around in the kitchen. His hand was on my knee, pushing me down next to him. I didn't think I could get up.

I hardly was able to get out here to the living room on my own as it was. I nearly fell over when I tried to get up from the dirty bed I was graced with.

Morgan had opened the door, demanding I join them, then left me to slowly make my way out. I didn't want to find out what would happen if I stayed lying there on the filthy mattress.

"I have to apologize for your mother's behavior; she's coming off a high," Morgan said as he leaned into me. I tried to lean away but ended up falling against him more than I wanted to.

"I wouldn't be in this mood if you'd just give me more," Joan yelled from the kitchen angrily.

"Jo," Morgan sighed, not pleased with her. "Come sit."

I closed my eyes as Joan came and took a seat, flopping down next to me, but far enough away that she wasn't touching me.

After a few minutes, I opened my eyes as Morgan coughed, clearing his throat. The movement made me feel queasy.

"Don't you dare get sick," Joan said with a glare my way.

"She can't help it. You know what the drugs do to us. It is so worth the relief from the pain," Morgan shrugged. "Come on, little girl. Let's at least get you to the bathroom."

I was surprised by his tenderness, like he cared about me. He lifted me softly up from the couch and carried me to the dirty bathroom. He barely sat me down on the floor before the little contents of my stomach came up.

Morgan made himself scarce.

WAKING UP COLD AND COVERED IN SWEAT, I FOUND MYSELF BACK on the mattress. I felt like death. I wished I had a blanket, but at least my clothes were still on.

The room was bathed in darkness, and I could hear loud music from, most likely, the living room. Voices floated to me, but I ignored them as much as I could. The door was closed, so I didn't think anyone would come bother me.

I was sore again, but I ignored it, moving slowly so I could try to reach my hidden phone. I needed out of here before Morgan tried to do anything.

I'd just touched the phone when the bedroom door was roughly pushed open and the music increased in volume. Groaning, I turned over, facing the intruder.

"Ah, my girl!" Morgan slurred as he flicked the light on. I squeezed my eyes shut against the brightness.

The sweet smell of pot reached my nose, and I tried to not to breathe in too deeply.

"Well, are you going to come join us? It's a party!" he said with a bright smile.

"No thanks," I said, faking a yawn, hoping he wouldn't push. I had never seen him high, and I didn't ever want to again. I hoped he'd drop it and forget all about me.

"Yes, come on," Morgan said as he walked towards me. I groaned as he lifted me by my upper arm.

"I don't want to see her," I mumbled as he pulled me behind him. I couldn't keep up, as my legs couldn't fully support my weight yet.

"Here she is," Morgan said, pushing me to sit on the couch. The room was filled with sweet-smelling smoke and my mother was lying flat on her back, looking happy and content. She only had her underwear and bra on.

"'Bout time," she smiled. "You've been asleep for two days now. It's time for you to earn your keep 'round here."

I had no idea how long it had been since the car accident. I wanted to go home.

"You are home," Morgan said, taking a seat next to me.

I must have spoken out loud.

"You are to stay here and help me. Joan doesn't meet all my needs," Morgan said, pulling me towards him by the arm he had wrapped around my shoulders.

"But Elijah," I said with tears in my eyes.

"He's not looking for you," Joan laughed. "He's dead. Gone. Poof!" She flung her arms up in the air, trying to make her words bigger than her voice.

"No!" I said, sitting up away from Morgan. He couldn't

BROKEN REVIVAL

be. He had to be alive, looking for me. I could feel my heart breaking as my breaths became heavier.

"I made sure he was dead," Joan said darkly. "He ruined our plans."

"No, please," I cried out, blinking back tears.

"He was in the way. If it wasn't for your father in the first place, I wouldn't have to be here now. He just had to ask questions because of the amount of time I was spending at the strip club," Joan went on.

"Breathe in, Dawn," Morgan said sweetly as he blew a breath full of smoke towards my face. Since I was panicking, I didn't think of holding my breath.

Coughing, I hunched over, not knowing what to do. I felt light headed again, but my panic seemed to calm somewhat.

"Good. Again," Morgan said, blowing more smoke into my face. "There ya go."

"No," I said weakly, trying to move away from him. I didn't want to be high. I didn't want anything he had to offer me. My body was weak, and now weaker in its relaxed state, as I tried to move as far away from him as I could.

He easily held me to him, making me breathe in more of the smoke. My body became as relaxed as it possibly could, and I was mostly leaning against him for support. I now understood why Joan was lying on the floor without a care in the world.

"Now you're more relaxed, it's past time to play," Morgan said with a glint in his eye. "All your pain is much more manageable, and you won't have such a trying let down when the drugs leave your system. You may have a slight headache and a dry mouth, but so much better all around."

"I want to go home," I whined. I really did want to go home, wherever that was—as long as it wasn't with Morgan.

"You are home, my sweets," Morgan laughed as he pressed a kiss to my cheek. His hand went to my knee, gently squeezing.

"No," I said weakly, trying to push his hand away as it crept up my thigh.

"Hush," he said, pressing his lips to mine harshly.

I was about to tell him to stop, but he stuck his slimy tongue into my mouth. I couldn't push him away.

"Get a room," Joan laughed.

"Gladly," Morgan said, breaking away from the kiss. With a lusty smile, he picked me up and took me back to my room, laying me down gently on the bed.

With a tenderness I didn't expect, he took my clothes off, and then his own. I lay there, unable to fight back.

"You are such . . . brightness," Morgan said, looking me up and down, taking in the curves of my body. I tried to wrap my arms around myself but he was too quick, pinning them at my sides. "Don't make me tie you up," he warned.

I nodded. I couldn't let him tie me up again. I had to make that phone call. I didn't know if what Joan said about Elijah was true or not, but I wasn't willing to let it deter me. I had to get out of here.

"You're too dry," Morgan nearly whined as he looked between my legs after spreading them open. He looked disappointed, and that made my gut twist in pain. "Stay." He left me there. I closed my eyes, praying he'd forget about me and just leave me be.

I must have dozed off, jumping as cold lube was squirted over my mound, dribbling down my butt crack. I opened my eyes with difficulty, looking up at him. He had a gleeful look on his face as he watched the lube slowly slide between my legs.

I shivered in disgust. He blew more smoke in my face, making me cough and try to turn my head again. Laughing, he used two fingers, swirling the lube around.

"I can't wait any longer," he moaned, moving to position himself so he could easily enter me. He leaned over my body.

He was way too warm, too heavy. "Stay still. I don't want to hurt you," he panted.

He roughly pushed himself into me. He must have lubed his dick up, too, as he easily slipped in. I could feel him press against my cervix, and I couldn't help but slightly cry out.

Even though he used lube, it still hurt. It hurt so much tears leaked from the corners of my eyes as he began to move in and out. He took what he wanted, not giving a damn about what I wanted.

"Shh. Daddy's got you. You're so tight," he moaned as his thrusts sped up. Bile rose in my throat.

I hated him.

I hated the fact he thought he could call himself *daddy*. As if raping their daughter was okay, but thinking I was his kid to do so. It was horrible to be raped by this man again.

He wasn't even my freaking father!

He pounded into me. The sound of slapping skin rang in my ears as he took me fast and hard.

I wanted him to stop.

I wanted it all to stop.

I couldn't take anymore. I couldn't!

I was crying for Elijah. I wanted his touch, his love. I just wanted Elijah.

Morgan didn't last long—maybe only a minute. I held my eyes closed, hoping he'd leave and never come back.

"Thank you, sweetie pie," he said, kissing me, before he gently removed himself. He left the room but came back, covering me with a blanket. "I'll be back for round two soon."

I waited until I heard loud snoring from the living room before I quietly moved to reach the phone. It took some work as I was tired, unsure if I was dreaming or not.

Listing to make sure no one was going to come my way, I turned my phone on, seeing many missed calls.

Clicking on one of them, I listened as it rang once. Twice.

"'Ello," answered a sleepy voice.

233

"Kaleb!"

~

ELIJAH

I hated hospitals. I loathed them and told everyone who would listen that I would never, ever be back in one.

It had been twenty-four hours since I'd been last given any type of pain meds or sedatives. It took a while for the drugs to leave my system, and it wasn't pleasant. I was grumpy for more than one reason.

I was more than happy to let Kaleb take care of me, even after all this time. We were the best of friends, and it was easy to let him take over for me. Plus, I wasn't in the state of mind to really give a damn.

I had woken up a few times panicking, wanting my girl, and Kaleb was there, calming me instantly. If it wasn't for him, I'd never be able to leave the hospital. Many times, when I woke up, it was with Kaleb touching me, almost in a loving manner, and it made me more confused, but calmed my thoughts at the same time.

I was now fully alert, finally five days after the accident, and being released with strict orders to take it easy, no drinking alcohol of any kind, and no driving, since my ribs were tender and my reflexes were slow due to the pain. I had refused any more pain meds, and that resulted in hardly any sleep.

I had tried to talk Kaleb into going home, but he refused to leave my side. My mother and father both came by a few times, but didn't stay long due to my attitude—not towards them, but everything else. I was angry I couldn't leave to search for my girl.

"Elijah," Kaleb warned me as I went to get out of bed. I was tired, sore, and I needed to move. I'd been stuck in bed for way too long, and I was hungry. Hungry for real food, not the crap the hospital called food.

"I'm fine," I glared at him, pushing myself slowly off the bed. My bare feet touched the cold floor. My legs were weak but manageable as I began to walk around the room like a caged animal.

"If you say so," Kaleb said, giving me a look that clearly said he knew I was pushing myself.

An hour later, I was finally released and seated in Kaleb's car, and too tired to fight about where he was taking me. My legs were weak and he'd had to help me get from the mandatory wheelchair into the car, not caring one bit about my grumbling.

"I'd turn you over my knee and spank you if it wasn't for the fact you're sore and learned your lesson already," Kaleb said sweetly as he drove off. I simply flipped him off, which making him to laugh at me again. I was sure he'd do just that if I wasn't in pain.

By the time we got to his house, I was almost in a daze. It took a little work to get me inside and to the couch since I plainly refused his help until I had nearly fallen over.

The girls were at Joslyn's house, not wanting to have the babies in the way and to let us sleep for a little while after coming here. I missed my Lizzy, but I was in no shape to care for her at that moment.

"Rest," Kaleb said with a tender kiss to my forehead, before he went to the chair, falling asleep before I could.

The ringing of a cell phone, Kaleb's, woke us both up to a darkened house. I groaned and rolled over as Kaleb answered it.

CHAPTER 31

DAWN

*L*oud banging noises and yelling woke me up sometime later. Everything was dark and I was extremely tired. I didn't want to move. My entire body was sore. I didn't know where the pain started and where it stopped.

Morgan had come back in and taken me as I lay there, almost lasting for what seemed liked forever. His cum coated my inner thigh, running down my core and cooling. It felt sticky as I kept my body still. My body was light and weak as he blew more smoke into my airways by kissing me. I didn't fight, didn't cry. I only hoped for freedom. Or death. I'd gladly take either one.

The banging continued and I groaned, trying to bury myself in the mattress and thin blanket covering me.

"What the hell do you think you're doing?" I heard Morgan shout at what sounded like the front door being kicked in.

I went to pull the covers closer to me, and I noticed that my phone was in my hands, dead.

I'd tried to call Kaleb, and I couldn't remember if it had gone through. I didn't think I'd survive here much longer.

I wouldn't see Elijah again, or Lizzy. I hadn't fought hard enough.

My heartbeat began to race and my eyes were clouded by tears.

The bedroom door was opened with a squeak, and I tried to hide under the cover, as small as I possibly could. I shook, unable to hide my fear or my panic. My body shivered violently.

As hurried footsteps came closer to me, I began to cry, tucking my chin into my chest further. I didn't want to be touched. Elijah had promised me he'd never let me get hurt, but he did. I wanted Elijah.

"Don't," I heard someone say right before the blanket was pulled back from me, and I couldn't help another huge shiver. The voice was hard and stern.

Footsteps retreated but someone was still in the room with me.

From the living room, I could hear Morgan yelling, crying almost. It wasn't clear what he was saying, and I didn't necessarily care.

"Hey, sweetheart," I heard the male voice say softly as he kneeled next to me. The voice sounded familiar. "You're safe now."

Unable to respond, I shook my head, crying out more than I already was. I was hyperventilating.

"Dawn," the voice said, closer, but calmly. There was no hint of anger or lust in his voice. "Please, can I help you?"

"Joan!" I heard Morgan yell out, shocked.

"I'm . . . sorry," I sobbed out, unable to comprehend what he wanted. Was he here to put me out of my pain?

"I'm going to touch you to wrap the blanket around you,

alright? We need to get you out of here," he said in an urgent voice.

When I didn't move more than I already had, he gently wrapped my form in the blanket, covering me the best he could. I jerked at his touch but he was careful, never touching my skin.

"I'm going to pick you up now, alright Dawn? I won't hurt you, I promise," he said. With a cry, afraid he was going to drop me since I was still in a ball, I wrapped my arms around his neck, hanging on for dear life. I kept my eyes clenched shut, my body tight.

"You're safe," he kept repeating as he began to walk, first out of the room, and then out of the house. I could smell smoke.

"I'll take her," said another voice as fire truck sirens came racing towards wherever I was. The person holding me tightened his grip.

"She won't be going anywhere without me," the one holding me said sternly. I cringed against him.

I felt him step up into a vehicle, then take a seat. I couldn't get my arms to loosen their grip around his neck. "It's okay, I got you, Dawn," he said in a whisper as he ran his hand down my back.

"Kaleb, we need her arm to start fluids," said another person, this one female. Her voice was calm and quiet.

Kaleb? He came?

"Dawn, can this nice lady start an IV in your arm?" the man—Kaleb—asked as he leaned his head on my own.

I shook, not knowing what to do. I heard him mumble something before another blanket was placed on me in a rush. It was warm, and the warmth soaked into my skin, into my bones.

"Kaleb?" I whispered, keeping my eyes closed. I could feel the vehicle we were in start to move and I clenched onto him tighter, if it were possible.

BROKEN REVIVAL

"I'm here, sweet girl," he said calmly. "You need to relax for me."

"I can't," I cried out, fearing this was just a dream. I was light headed. "Elijah?"

"He's safe," Kaleb said. And that's all I needed to hear to allow my body descend into darkness.

~

I FELT A HEAVINESS IN ALL MY LIMBS AND I COULDN'T SEEM TO move anything but my fingers. When I did, something warm and strong squeezed back on both sides. My eyes were closed, but I could feel the warmth of the sun across my body.

The beeping of a machine reached my ears in the quietness of the room. I could hear muted voices from somewhere, but wasn't sure if they were nearby or miles away.

"She'll have a full recovery, but she needs an OBGYN as soon as she's up to it," said a voice from somewhere. Were they talking about me? "I did a rape kit, and it came back positive. According to the files from the doctor she saw just a few weeks ago, she is able to have kids, but it's low risk for her to get pregnant since she hasn't had a normal menstrual cycle for years. She needs to get on the pill to help re-start it. I can give her the Plan B pill to make sure she didn't get pregnant.

"The accident broke one of her ribs, so there is bruising around that area, and they will be longer lasting than the others. The swelling on her face will slowly go down, but ice it a few times a day if needed," the doctor said quietly. "She could benefit from seeing a psychologist, possibly long term. Overall, she seems to be in pretty decent shape."

"Thank you," I heard Kaleb say quietly from beside me.

"And you, Elijah, need to get some rest. You really aren't in much better shape," the doctor said lightly.

"Yeah, yeah," Elijah said from the other side of me.

"Take care," the doctor said, before leaving.

I was just about to doze off again when Kaleb spoke up. "How are you holding up?" He sounded tired himself.

"Don't even try, Kaleb," Elijah said, just as tiredly. His voice was coarse and sounded worn out.

"I'm only asking," Kaleb replied calmly.

I wanted to open my eyes, to move, to grunt something. My heart soared at the thought that Elijah was safe, and alive. I wanted to dance if I could just get my body to move, but it wouldn't cooperate.

Breathing in and out, I let sleep claim me again.

∼

"PLEASE, DAWN, WAKE UP FOR ME, SWEETHEART," I HEARD Elijah beg as I felt his head against my arm.

"She'll wake up when she's ready," Kaleb sighed as he moved into a more comfortable position. "And she may not want you touchin' her when she does."

"Don't you dare," Elijah said, and I could feel the tension between the two sweep over me

"Stop," I managed to get out. I wasn't sure it came out clear, but I squeezed Elijah's hand as tightly as I could.

"Oh, Dawn. Thank God," Elijah said, near tears.

I slowly forced my eyes open, glad there was no bright light above me. Blinking, I looked over at Elijah first, seeing how tired he looked. His forehead had a few stitches. His eyes were sunken in, and I had to wonder what had happened to him, before remembering we were in the same car accident.

I turned to Kaleb, who looked just as tired, but not as banged up. "You came." My voice was no more than a whisper, but I was in awe. He had saved me.

"Of course, little sis," Kaleb smiled at me. His smile was filled with love, and I truly felt like he was my big brother.

"When can I go home?" I asked, looking between both of

them. I wanted to be held and never let go. I wanted to see my daughter.

"Probably tomorrow afternoon," Elijah said, giving Kaleb a look that said to get lost.

"And that's my queue to make those phone calls," Kaleb said, standing up. "Just yell if you need me, Dawn."

"Thanks, Kaleb," I replied, taking a deep breath and letting go of his hand.

"Do you remember what happened?" Elijah asked once Kaleb had closed the door behind him.

"Most of it. I remember the crash, then waking up wherever Morgan took me, and almost everything he did. He drugged me, trying to lessen my pain, but it backfired and made me sick. Then he got me high off pot smoke. He raped me, Elijah," I answered in tears. "I was able to hide my phone but wasn't able to call anyone until after I knew it was safe to do it. I was so scared."

"Hey, it's okay. You're safe now, Dawn," Elijah soothed me. He touched my face gently, and I let his warmth soak into me.

"Joan set the house on fire when she heard the sirens, and Kaleb got there just in time," he went on. "You wouldn't let the firefighters touch you, or even get near you. They were all trying to get you out first, knowing you were missing.

"The house was a total loss, due to water and smoke damage. Of course, it wasn't worth saving, anyway. Joan was high when she started the fire. She didn't make it."

"Morgan?" I asked, needing to know what happened to him.

"He's in jail, without bail, on twenty-four-hour watch," he answered. "The court date won't be set for some time, but with all the evidence against him, he'll never make it out alive."

∽

"Dawn Ellis, correct?" said a woman as she entered the room. Her blond hair was neatly pulled back into a ponytail. Elijah slowly moved back, so it wouldn't seem like he was overwhelming me.

"Uh . . ." I said, drawing a blank.

"What can I help you with, Dr?" Elijah asked, sitting up straighter so he wasn't lying near my arm.

"I'd like to talk to Dawn alone for a moment,' she answered.

"No," I said, instantly alert. No one was going to take him away again. They couldn't. "Please, no."

"Okay, he can stay, but I still need to talk to you. I'm Dr. Mai," she said soothingly, taking the chair Kaleb had sat in and moving it away from the bed a few feet. "I only want to talk."

At my nod, she began. "Anything you say is just between us, and will not leave this room. I understand you have been through a great deal, and it must have taken its toll on you and the ones you love. I am here to listen if you ever need to talk."

"I have Elijah, and Kaleb, and our family," I replied. Everyone who mattered knew what I had been through.

"Well, this is what I do, so if you change your mind, just give me a call anytime. Here's my card," she said, laying it on the food tray before making her way out of the room.

"Are you okay?" Elijah asked, scooting back as close as he possibly could.

"I will be," I said tiredly. "Hold me?"

"Always," he said as I scooted over on the little bed, making enough room for him. I wrapped my body around him, not caring how much pain I was in.

"Do you want to take a precaution against being pregnant from Morgan?" Elijah asked.

"There's no point. He can't have any kids," I sighed, closing my eyes. "I love you, Elijah. Forever."

CHAPTER 32

DAWN

*G*etting back into a calm and stress-free routine was easier said than done. That first week after thinking Elijah was dead, killed by the person who'd given birth to me, and finding him alive—a little banged up, but well and alive—I didn't want him out of my sight. I had to be touching him almost all the time.

Emily had talked me down from being so clingy with him. She understood why, but she was right. I was afraid he'd disappear at any moment. I finally ended up taking a long, calming bath, knowing Elijah would still be there when I got out.

Our bruises slowly faded, and after a month, we were back to our original selves. Lizzy was growing, and Kelly and I got together at least once a week so our daughters could play together.

Joslyn and Vence took care of Lizzy once a month to allow us to have some time alone. Elijah hadn't gone back to work.

He had chosen to stay at home after everything that had happened to us.

I was finally figuring out who I was, and what I wanted, for the most part, not afraid to state my ideas or ask my questions. Elijah didn't often challenge me, mostly because we had the same ideas and likes.

I got back into the habit of cleaning and keeping the house. I knew Joslyn did her own home, and Kelly did hers most of the time, so I decided to do ours. This, of course, led to Elijah questioning me.

"You don't have to keep the house anymore. I can hire someone to do that," Elijah said, watching me dust the entertainment center while Lizzy took a nap.

"I don't mind, Elijah," I said truthfully. "I actually like to clean. It's soothing. Plus, you like to watch me," I said with a smile.

"Yes, I do, but I can watch you just sit, too," he said with a smirk. "I can find something better for you to do—something more entertaining."

"Elijah," I sighed with a light laugh and shook my head. "Just let me clean. We live together, have a daughter, and hopefully, will have more within the next few years."

"Really?" he asked, shocked. I guess I hadn't really confirmed if I wanted more kids one way or another since the whole Morgan situation. I had finally started on birth control pills to start up my periods again. It was a step in the right direction. I also had to go back into the doctor in five months to make sure I hadn't come down with HIV or hepatitis, just to be on the safe side. Who knew where Morgan or Joan had been? I didn't truly think I'd end up with anything, but I wanted to be safe rather than sorry.

"Yes, if you still want to. It could take up to a year to make sure I'm regular, but yeah," I said with a happy smile.

"Of course I do!" Elijah exclaimed. "First, we need to make a change for the better."

I hadn't moved from my spot by the TV, where I was attempting to dust, when Elijah got up with a look of hope and nervousness in his eyes. With a calm face and a deep breath in, he bent to one knee, looking up at me.

"I want us to be a family, not just by living together, but by becoming one—becoming whole. I love you, Dawn Ellis. Will you marry me?" he asked.

"Yes," I answered, not having to think about it. Tears gathered in my eyes as I swung my arms around his neck, kissing him with everything I had in me.

"I'm sorry I don't have a ring yet, but I will get you one soon," he promised between kisses.

"I'm not picky," I said happily, as we leaned back from one another, and looked into each other's eyes.

"I know you aren't." He hugged me tightly again, right as a cry from Lizzy sounded through the monitor.

The following day, before we went to the family dinner at his parents' house, we went ring shopping. I found and fell in love with a very simple white gold ring. It had small diamonds around the top half, bright and shiny, while the bottom half was smooth. The entire ring was thin and fit my finger perfectly, so we didn't even have to wait for resizing.

To say that Joslyn was surprised was an understatement. She was already talking about wedding plans and ideas.

"We want to be married in the summer so we can have the reception outside," Elijah said, bringing me closer as we sat on the couch. "And nothing fancy. Just simple, and short. It will give Emily time to get back in shape, too, after having her little one."

"Mandy won't be happy about that," Vence laughed. "She's been planning since she met you, Dawn."

"I don't want to go all out," I said. "I do have a dress in mind already, so Joslyn, if you and Emily could be in charge of the decorations, maybe?" I asked, not knowing what to do about that part.

"Oh, I would love too!" Emily said. She was due in two months, so an August wedding would give us plenty of time to figure out the details I didn't want to deal with.

"Me too," Joslyn said, giving me a side hug.

Most of the talk between us girls was about the wedding and what I thought I may want. I really didn't care about the colors or the decorations, as long as I got to pick out the wedding dress I wanted. I had seen this wonderful lace dress that was long, and perfect, that would show off my curves. I just hoped to find something in white, instead of the dark blue showcased in the advert.

After getting back home that night, I brought up a subject we hadn't talked about since before the accident. I knew Morgan's trial wouldn't start until later next month, and I got out of having to face him by giving a detective copies of the journals I had written. In them was all the abuse I had been forced to endure, and enough evidence was written and signed by me to allow me not to have to show up in the courts, as long as Morgan's lawyer didn't demand my presence. Even the D.A. was confident that the judge would take my journals and affidavit as my testimony, to save me from having to face him again.

"Is the offer Kaleb mentioned still up?" I asked shyly as I did the dishes left from lunch. Lizzy was banging on the chairs, walking from one to the next as she held on.

"What offer?" Elijah asked, tilting his head to the side.

"Having a scene for us? Well, for me?" I asked, feeling embarrassed at having to ask. I was ready. Knowing what to expect while in the playroom would help me. I needed to let Elijah have some sort of control over something, since he hardly took control of anything else I did these days.

"I'm sure it is," Elijah drawled with a lazy smile. "Are you sure?"

"Yeah." I said, hoping he'd go along with me and let me

do this my way. The idea was thrilling and I really wanted to try.

"Okay, I'll set it up the next time that Lizzy goes to my parents' house," he replied after a short pause. He looked at me, gauging my reactions before he'd answered.

"Thank you!" I said, flinging my arms around him, kissing him hard. He easily let me take control . . . for a moment. With Lizzy awake, we couldn't dare take it any further.

∼

ELIJAH

I was surprised Dawn was ready for more action in the bedroom, and I couldn't deny her more than I had been already. I hadn't wanted to take anything further due to the fact we were still healing, and I just wanted to enjoy the feeling of us together.

I had called Kaleb later that day and he was all for it, saying he'd call his parents, who'd been bugging them for quite some time to keep Lilly, so it wasn't an issue.

I was excited, as it had been way too long since I'd seen anyone scene. The club that I used to go to had different couples who would scene weekly. Since the case took up most of my spare time, and now, I wanted to spend any extra with Dawn and Lizzy, I didn't want to spend any at the club anymore.

"Hey girly," Kaleb said towards my girl as they entered the house later that week. Kelly smiled at us before making her way upstairs to get into sub mode. She always had to take just a few minutes to get into the right mindframe.

"You can always call red if you want us to stop. This won't be about our pleasure. It's about you seeing and understanding how it all works. I will more be explaining what things are as we go along, and how this type of relationship works, than really showing anything at this time," Kaleb went on as he took a seat by my girl. "If you have questions, I would be more than willing to answer anything, and so will Elijah."

"Okay," Dawn answered, wide-eyed, but with wonder.

I had never let anyone in my playroom other than myself and Dawn. I hadn't even let a one-nighter go there, let alone anywhere near my home.

When we got upstairs, Dawn was holding my hand for dear life, both girls took a seat on the couch.

"Good, kitten," Kaleb said as he entered the room behind us. "Just to clarify, we are showing Dawn how certain toys can cause certain reactions—certain pleasures." He circled his wife, touching her downcast face. "This will give her a good look, an idea of what each thing is. I won't be using anything that will make anyone cringe, just the basic items that are great to for beginners."

He turned towards the bag of items Kelly had placed on the bed. I moved Dawn by the hand to the chair on the other side of the room. It'd give her a chance to look and watch, but not seem like we were intruding on something.

"Are you familiar with vibrators, Dawn?" Kaleb asked, holding up a similar one to the one I had introduced to her before. He stood on the other side of the coffee table with his bag in front of him.

"Yes," she answered in a stronger voice that I expected. I figured she'd be afraid to talk, much less answer anything. I couldn't help but beam at her.

"Good. So you know they can bring pleasure in many ways. If, let's say, you put it on your nipples, it can help bring them to hard peaks. There are many different types. Some are as simple as this one," Kaleb went on, looking at my girl but holding no lust for her. He was in teacher mode. He held up a jelly vibrator. "This is the simplest of the styles. There are some that have wands attached to the front, which will put pressure on your clit. They come in all types, sizes, and variety. Everyone likes something different, and I'm sure Elijah has a few types you can both play around with to find out which ones you like best. Kelly, on another day, can even talk to you about what she likes and doesn't like to help you get an idea."

He sat down the toy before picking up another thing. One that made me cringe at just the sight.

"Now, these are nipple clamps. They are, for the most part, all the same, but some vibrate, and some can send a small shockwave. They can bring pleasure and pain at the same time. Not all women, or men, like them, but Elijah loved this particular set," Kaleb winked, making me to laugh.

"There's also all sorts of styles of ropes, and they can each bring on pleasure by being bound in a certain way. Most Doms love to see their subs tied up and helpless, unable to do anything but stay in whatever position they are placed in."

"We also don't always just limit our play time to a playroom. We play at least once a week, sometimes more if we want to. We don't always bring the submissive and dominant into play—only when we feel the need to. Some couples like to Dom/sub 24/7, while others only during certain times. It's all up to the couple, and what works best for them," he went on, letting go of Kelly's hands. She slowly let them drop back to her sides, but otherwise didn't move or make another sound. "Do you have any questions?"

Dawn shook her head. We had agreed they wouldn't take it too far, since I didn't want to scare her off. I had been a whirlwind of emotions after first finding out about most of the same items.

"Good. So there are different types of punishment, and the same goes for them as the toys. Some of the items like a whip, cane, paddle, and even just a regular hand can bring pleasure. The hand is one of our favorites, and Kelly has gotten that a number of times," Kaleb said with a smile. "The paddle isn't bad, either. The cane is the worst, or the belt, which I never use, but you always do warm ups with the hand before using any of those items."

"Neither will I," I said in her ear. "You may end up liking my hand, though."

"Once you are up to it, you two will have to go to the club and see a few acts, and just get a feel of what you may want to try someday," Kaleb said. "If you ever need someone to answer anything, both Kelly and I would be more than willing to try and answer your questions, and so will Elijah. I'm sure the books in his office would come in handy, too.

"We'd do a whole scene, but it is a lot to take in. The first step is to know what is expected, what the toys are, and how one is able to respond to them. A wonderful Dom will know how far to take it, what buttons to push, and when to back off. A submissive needs to know how to communicate with her Dom at all times. It's not just about pleasure or pain. It's about becoming someone who can release each other's stresses, and helping one another be one together," Kaleb said.

"The aftercare is important, and Elijah knows that. That is the time to make sure there are no lasting marks and to make sure to rub or put salve on any tender spots. It also gives the sub time to come back to earth in her own time, so as not to be rushed. Sometimes it takes longer than others. It all depends on what the scene is, and how much pleasure and pain was brought on," Kaleb went on.

Kaleb then went on to explain some of the other items in the playroom, like the spanking bench and the St. Andrew's Cross, and what roles they could be used for.

"The items for pain can also be used for pleasure, and vice versa. Some Doms may deny the pleasure of coming, or may prolong it, for more pleasure, I know Kelly loves when I do this on occasion." Kaleb went on. "Sometimes Doms will not allow a sub to come as a form of punishment, but it is wonderful when one finally can, after a few days of being denied."

"The Dom is not the one that holds all the control. The sub also holds a great amount of control by what we communicate to our Doms."

They both left shortly afterward, and Dawn was deep in thought. She went straight to my office, where I gave her the beginner's book into my lifestyle. I printed off a contract, telling her to use whatever she needed to learn about the things included. She was welcome to use any of the books, the internet, or even coming to either Kaleb, Kelly or myself with any questions.

I took off all my hard limits, since there was no way I would even let her consider them.

CHAPTER 33

DAWN

A week later, after reading through a great number of Elijah's books, we had come to a conclusion of my soft and hard limits, along with a few things I was willing to try. I didn't mind vibrators and some bondage. I was curious about anal play and penetration but wasn't sure if I would like it. But I wanted to give Elijah something that hadn't been taken from me before.

Most of the things on the contract seemed easy to do and easy to understand. Fisting was off the list for sure, since it sounded painful, along with figging, flogging, gunplay, and hogties, to name just a few.

I was looking forward to the bondage, as long as music was playing softly in the background. I thought I would be just fine. Elijah would be my Master in the playroom, but only after we got used to the idea of us being together in that environment.

We'd also not take it into the playroom until after I was able to handle it in the bedroom, which was my idea. No matter how much I wanted to just jump in and play, I knew we had to take baby steps to get to that point.

The night that Kaleb and Kelly helped me to understand what was expected, and what kinds of toys there were, Elijah let me pick out a toy to try other than the vibrator. He wanted to take my mind off what I was trying desperately to absorb.

I knew this lifestyle was not for couples who wanted a reason to beat the people they loved. BDSM was a lifestyle, inside and out of the bedroom. It was to bring pleasure to one another and make the sex more fun between the two. So many people, mostly the new ones to the scene, didn't know the concept, thinking it was perfectly normal for any man to beat the crap out of their partner. It wasn't okay. It took a lot of communication and research on both parties to know what to expect.

Elijah, with a calm demeanor, led me to a drawer full of different vibrators. They were all about the same size, but a few were longer than others.

"Pick one out you'd like to play with today," he'd said, moving behind me to kiss my neck gently.

Looking at them, I had no idea which one to pick. Some had the clit massager, a few had an anal massager, some were ribbed, and some were plain.

"I don't know," I said, looking but not touching.

"Well, there are the normal everyday ones, like the one I used on you at the pool, or the ones that rub your clit, while hitting that spot inside you, or the ones that massage your butt, but don't insert into you. I have the ones that hit all three spots, but I'm sure you aren't up to that yet. It can be very pleasurable once you get used to the feeling. The first time can be overwhelming for anyone," he drawled in a husky voice.

I took a deep breath, then picked one from the middle. It was a light blue vibrator that seemed to have a few girths to it. It wasn't as smooth as the one that Elijah had used last time. It was a little longer, but not by much. I handed it to Elijah, who only smiled before leading me towards the bedroom.

"This is not a scene, but in most cases, while in scene, a sub must have permission to speak. I will not require that of you until you are more comfortable being in sub mode. You are free, always, to speak, to ask questions or make any noises you want to," he said once we entered the bedroom. "There are three safe words: green, for good, yellow, for when I am pushing a limit, and red, when you want me to stop. I will ask you your color, and I expect you to answer accordingly to how you feel."

"Yes, Sir," I answered, looking up at him. I took in everything he had to say.

After tossing the toy on the bed and turning on some low music, he moved towards me where I stood frozen. He gently and lovingly moved his hand up to my cheeks, then brought his mouth down to meet mine. I stood on my tip toes, reaching his soft, warm lips. I couldn't help but moan into him.

Slowly, we began to play a song with our lips, moving in sync together, reaching everywhere we could. My hands ended up in his hair, pulling lightly as our kiss intensified.

Breaking away to breathe, Elijah's eyes were alight with lust.

"I'm not gonna be able to last, since it's been a little bit. I want you to suck me off so I can hold out to make you orgasm when we fuck," he said, unzipping his pants.

I kneeled and took him into my mouth once his cock was free. He was already hard and dripping with pre-cum.

I licked him, wetting him with my saliva before taking him all the way in with one smooth stroke. He moaned deeply when my nose was right against his pubic bone.

I began to suck on him slowly, hollowing out my cheeks as

he slid down my throat. I licked the underside of him, knowing he liked it.

With one of my hands, I moved up towards his balls, massaging and rolling them gently.

It didn't take him long to come, squirting down my throat. I swallowed all he gave me.

I let him softly pop out of my mouth, smiling up at him, pleased with myself. I was getting better each time I sucked him off, and couldn't wait to do it again.

"Good God, Dawn," he breathed out, looking down at me, satisfied. "I'm gonna have to make sure you feel as good as you just made me. Hop up on the bed and lie on your back."

Smiling, I stood up. Instead of moving to the bed, I decided to strip, slowly, in front of Elijah. I lifted the tank top over my head first, then moved to my pants. I stood there in only a bra, knowing I wouldn't be needing underwear that night anyway. The last thing I took off was my bra, leaving me naked and bare in front of my love.

"Wow," Elijah said, looking at me up and down and not moving. "I think you enjoyed that a little too much."

"Do you like?" I asked, turning in a circle. I couldn't help but give my butt a little wiggle.

"Very much so," he said, spanking my ass cheeks sharply. I yelped out at him in surprise. "Now, up on the bed, miss."

I was on the bed in a heartbeat. Elijah shook his head with a smile before stalking towards me with a look in his eyes. He was hungry, and he was going to devour me.

I was laid out, hands up by my head, my legs slightly parted. I looked up at him in a lust filled daze. I never knew talking about toys and bringing someone pleasure alone could turn me on so much. I could feel the drip of my wetness between my legs, coating my asshole, almost tickling in a way.

"You're wet," Elijah said. I smiled shyly at him. Of course I was. "You are so responsive."

Slowly, he brought his hands up to my feet, gently and firmly rubbing them, making the stress disappear. He worked on my toes, bringing me pleasure I didn't know was there. I closed my eyes, enjoying the feeling of his hands on my body as he worked his way up my calves, thighs, hips, arms, and shoulders. He completely ignored the places I wanted his hands; my pussy and breasts were begging for attention.

He made sure he massaged each place completely before he finally brought his hands to my tits. He started on the sides, gently swiping his hands along the outside of them, under them, and on top, before finally touching my peaks that were desperate for his attention. I moaned out as he pinched them tightly. I arched into him, wanting more, anything, as long his hands never left my body.

After a few minutes of pinching and massaging, I was almost to my climax when he stopped. I never knew nipple play could bring one so much pleasure. I whined as he moved his hands away, moving them down my body.

"Patience, my girl," he said with a smile, knowing exactly what he was doing.

Finally, after a long moment, he began to run his hands up and down my inner thighs, making me ache for more. I was ready to burst and it wouldn't take me long at all.

"I'm going to use this." He grabbed the toy I had picked out. "I don't want you to come . . . yet. Try to hold on as long as you can."

I nodded my head, letting him know I understood.

"Color?" he asked, turning the vibrator on.

"Green, Sir," I answered without thought.

He gently inserted the vibrator into my slick heat, and I involuntarily bucked against it, seeking more friction. I could feel the difference right away from the other one we'd used. This one was just a little bit fuller and longer—not nearly as long as he was, but was very enjoyable. I could feel the ridges on it.

BROKEN REVIVAL

He kept it on low, knowing it wouldn't take much to bring me release. He slowly pumped it in and out, watching me. I could feel his eyes on me, taking me in eagerly.

"I can't . . ." I panted out, on the verge of climax.

He knew, too. He gently removed it, letting me calm down a moment before he crawled on top of me, lining himself up. The tip of his cock entered me but he didn't push in, even though I arched into him, trying to take him in all the way.

"Hold on tight," he said as he roughly sheathed himself inside me after putting on a condom. "You are so wet," he panted, giving me a moment to get used to him.

"I'm so close, Elijah," I moaned, trying to buck into him. I needed to cum. I needed him to move.

I needed more.

"Come as much you want," he said as he began to slide in and out, fast. I came instantly, crying out in pleasure as he continued roughly banging into me.

Before my orgasm was finished, he brought me up again, lighting the fire in my lower belly as he hit my g-spot over and over. On my third time, he came with me, groaning loud and long as I squeezed everything out of him.

He took care of me afterward, making sure I was clean before cuddling together as we slept. I was happy and content, and couldn't wait for more time together. I would always crave him, no matter what.

EPILOGUE

DAWN

I couldn't believe we've been together for a year. So much had changed in such a short amount of time. No one could have been able to tell me I'd have gone from a sex slave to a respected woman. No one could have told me that I'd be in love.

I never knew what love was until Elijah came into my life.

Now, after finally figuring out what love was, and how life would be enjoyed, I couldn't wait to live life to the fullest. I couldn't wait to be a part of life that brought new adventures inside and out of the house.

I wanted a family. I wanted kids of my own. But most of all, I wanted to *live*.

Currently, I was laying on the bed. My hands were above my head, holding on the silky rope tightly as my husband teased me. I was soaking wet, and wanted so much more.

"What color are you?" Elijah asked as he moved around the bed.

"Green, Sir," I said, keeping my eyes on him as he moved

back to the side of the bed and grabbed the bullet vibrator and testing the remote before coming back near me on the bed this time. He leaned on his knees beside me.

"Excellent," he grinned as he brought the vibrator to my lower lips, teasing me and making me crave more. I smiled, remembering the first time we had used this very vibrator. After a minute of teasing me, he slowly pushed it in, and I moaned at the fullness. I knew I would be even fuller by the time he'd put his cock into me.

"Please, Sir," I whined. The bullet was on the lowest setting, creating a nice warm feeling in my lower belly, but not nearly enough at the same time.

He left it there as he gently spread my legs apart further, so he could see his handy work. He licked his lips before grabbing the remote and turning it up a notch. I almost wanted to say he could tie my feet to the end posts, but wasn't sure if I would be able to handle it. Instead, I turned my focus back to the pleasure at hand.

"Need more?" he smirked, already knowing the answer. I eagerly nodded, enjoying the sensations. He turned it up another notch before covering my mouth with his own. His lips were soft and hard at the same time, and I moaned into him, trying to touch him everywhere I possibly could. It wouldn't take much more to get me over the edge.

Our tongues battled, trying to win some sort of dominance duel. Elijah pulled back, breathless. His eyes were filled with lust and love. His gentle hands went to my breasts, tweaking the hardened nipples to the point of pain. He sucked the right one into his warm, wet mouth while he played with my left. I moaned, closing my eyes and letting my head lie back on the pillow.

Somewhere along with the pleasure he brought me, he had lost his boxers. "Are you ready for me?" he asked, pulling the vibrator out and lining himself up. I was so close.

I could feel him right there, right where I wanted and needed him as he teased me again.

"Yes," I answered, knowing he wouldn't do anything until I gave the okay to do so.

He didn't wait any longer. He pushed my legs up, bending my knees and spread me wide before he lined himself up with my entrance and shoved his cock all the way in me, in one forceful move, filling me, marking me as his. I loved the feeling of his cock in me, and I knew I would want him in other places one day.

"Fuck, baby. This might be over before I move, if your fucking walls grip my cock any harder," he groaned, closing his eyes at the sensation.

He only waited a short moment before moving, hitting the place that brought me the most pleasure. He went slowly at first, drawing it out, making me crave more and more. In. Pause. Out. Pause. In. Pause. Repeat.

"Faster please, Sir?" I asked, breathless, begging with my eyes on him as he slowly moved inside of me.

He complied, moving faster and harder. I could tell he was close, and I involuntarily clenched around him, causing him to moan as he pumped into me.

"Harder, please, Sir," I begged.

As his thrusts increased in speed, it brought me closer and closer to the edge as he hit me in just the right place.

"Come for me," he panted out. It took me only another moment as we came together and stars exploded behind my closed eyelids. He slowed down, letting our connection continue as the after effects slowed.

"Wow," I said, opening my eyes and grinning from below him once I caught my breath.

"Wow indeed," he smiled in return, as he pulled out of me. I wanted to stay like that forever if it was possible.

Made in the USA
Columbia, SC
27 October 2017